THE STRUCTURE OF REALITY

DR. J. MICHAEL STRAWN

Meme from Representational Research artist Elizabeth Darnell. For information about terms, see the Glossary at RepresentationalResearch.com.

THE STRUCTURE OF REALITY

DR. J. MICHAEL STRAWN

Jeannie Pace, editor

Illustrations by Elizabeth Darnell

RepresentationalResearch.com

Published by RepresentationalResearch.com

ISBN: 978-1-0880-1179-9

Publisher's Introduction

Which reality is real?

This question has existed for ages, as people wondered if what they felt *inside* was more real than what they and others could observe and perhaps even agree about, on the *outside.*

That issue: what's inside a person, versus what's outside. Two realities.

That's come to the forefront of postmodern culture as the perceptions of the individual are being enthroned as "my reality" by the individual, despite the conflicting "realities" of other individuals, and what some might call "external reality" of the world of facts and things.

That issue expanded: what's inside person "A" versus what's inside all others, versus in most cases what's perceivable outside. Three realities.

Now there's a new reality wrinkle: the Metaverse. It's an outgrowth of many types of media that have begun to swallow up the consciousness of individuals. But now people are being offered a fourth "reality," the much more comprehensive so-called Metaverse, which can take elements of seen reality and enfold them into a digital fantasy "reality." This false reality engulfs the consciousness by means of incredible, lifelike computer graphics aiming to at least partially replace in the minds of people the physical reality in which their bodies move and operate.

Thus, yet another "reality:" Digital reality versus physical reality.

But these issues, these ideas of comparative "realities," are eclipsed for the Bible believer in a much bigger picture. As portrayed in the Bible, there is only one reality: *the part you can see* (and perceive autonomously or with others) compared with *the part of reality you can't see:* what God knows with infinite access to the past, present and future. How He assesses from His vantage point, unseen. And wonder of wonders, what He chooses to share with people in a very specific way. That's the third part of reality, that God links the unseen to the seen by means of His Word.

The true, complete issue: The seen versus the unseen.

- *The Seen = all human perceptions of both inside and outside conditions,*

versus

- *The Unseen = the realm of God and His power,*

plus

- *The Link = the connection originating in the unseen (the Bible) that makes the unseen knownable*

Yes, there is a need to know what God wants to tell people about the true nature of reality! And this book, addressing that need, is at the end of a process of teaching by a renowned thinker.

In 2015, minister Alfredo Pineda saw a need. Though Dr. J. Michael Strawn, a mentor to thousands, was proficient at in-depth lessons, a new generation of people respond well to shorter messages. Pineda asked Dr. Strawn if he would prepare short paragraphs to send by text message to help build faith and confidence in the Bible. Soon others wanted these text messages, and the list has grown over the years to include email recipients too. The messages are terse and to the point. Strawn insists on biblical basis for what he writes and teaches, using the Bible as agent when dealing with all matters sociological – as patient.[1]

1. Search on *RepresentationalResearch.com* in the Glossary for "agent-patient" or any other unfamiliar terms in this book.

These *Structure of Reality* short lessons first appeared as a series of text/email weekday messages in 2021. They have been minimally edited and preserve some of the limitations of text messages (no italics, for instance, although a few have been added in editing.)

The lessons address the individual books of the Bible, generalizing (more about that later) from Scripture to extract what the Holy Spirit has breathed into each book about the nature of reality. And certainly few subjects are more timely than this, since the supposition of "personal reality" and "personal truth" are so pervasive in our culture.

Dr. Strawn has been writing and teaching for decades. He is the originator of the field of Representational Research, first birthed at Trinity Southwest University and continuously archived at RepresentationalResearch.com. Some of his most well-known Biblical concepts are the Three-D Model of Reality, the Phases of Faith, and the practice of generalizing from Scripture.

Briefly stated, a generalization is parallel language to the Text (not just rewording it.) Any valid generalization is true to the passage in question and the generalization will be true all throughout Scripture. One of Strawn's most well-known generalizations from the passage about David and Goliath, for instance, is "Material circumstances do not determine outcomes." Each of the following lessons provides generalizations, and in the workbook section invites you to explore some on your own.

This is meat, not milk: lessons for real Bible learners not just theologians. The lessons can be read in any order; if, for instance, one's current interest lies in a particular New Testament book. However, please read the Genesis item as foundational. All the lessons are excellent sources of material for sermons; for dissent groups and other small group study; or just as many presently use them, for regular daily Bible study.

Blessed reading to you.

Author's Introduction: The Nature of Reality

1. Worldview is the attempt to capture the nature of any human collective and its institutions. My problem with worldview is that the categories by which it is developed are mostly derivable from the academic discipline of anthropology.
2. But the Bible largely deals with THE STRUCTURE OF REALITY.
3. Page after biblical page, the reader is presented with a structure of real things.
4. Accordingly, then, from the Bible, what is called "REALITY", is composed of 3 individual parts: (1) That which is invisible. Although God is invisible, that does not affect His existence. He is as real as a rock! Nor is He an abstraction. (2) That which is visible, quantifiable, what we routinely refer to as real, is the second part of the COMPLEX OF REALITY. (3) There is an index or a linkage between the two. Scripturally, that index is twofold: linguistic revelation and supernatural power.
5. It becomes quite noticeable that much of what we call thought, speech and behavior is a response to what we perceive to be "reality".
6. The behavior of the Israelites during the Exodus—their serial failures of faith were always founded upon their incomplete comprehension of the STRUCTURE OF REALITY.
7. To them "REALITY" was one-dimensional, consisting uniquely of tangible materiality. But biblically, that won't do. Beginning in Genesis, it is stipulated that the visible part of reality was *resultant* and not at all causal.
8. Materiality is not independent of the INVISIBLE CAUSAL PART OF REALITY. We live in a Cause ➡ to EFFECT UNIVERSE.
9. And all CAUSATION IS THE PROPRIETARY FUNCTION OF THE GOD OF THE BIBLE.
10. It turns out that in some non-trivial ways, some churches have reduced the realm of faith to doctrinal practice! However, it is possible to hold to right doctrine and yet, miss the greater STRUCTURE OF REALITY. Therefore, doctrinal practice is not the essence of faith. We must try to transcend RATIONAL LIMITS artificially put on biblical faith. For biblical faith carries the reader beyond RATIONAL LIMITS.

Reflecting on Genesis[1]:

What's the Main Point or Generalization this Lesson makes About Reality in this Book of the Bible?

CHANGEPOINTS

I think I need to change my view of reality to match God's in the following areas:

Make a list here of other verses in the book that deal with God's view of reality

1

2

3

4

5

6

7

8

1. To see how one student filled out this page for the book of Habakkuk, see the example at the end of the book.

From Genesis

THE STRUCTURE OF REALITY

1. REALITY IS COMPOSED OF THREE PARTS: (1)THE PART THAT WE CAN SEE; THE TEMPORAL (2) THAT PART THAT WE CANNOT SEE; THE SPIRITUAL AND (3) THE LINK BETWEEN THE TWO.
2. Every component of reality is rooted in God, "In the beginning God created the heavens and the earth".
3. Spiritual reality precedes Temporal Reality, 1:26.
4. Man occupies the top tier of the reality hierarchy, 1:28.
5. God commands men in time and materiality, 2:16.
6. Cain was among the first generations of men that did not understand the structure of reality nor did he obey it. 4:1-10.
7. The favor of the Lord bestowed upon men, in time and materiality, must equally be considered to be a category of reality, 6:8.
8. The spiritual Reality is Causal, and Temporal Reality is resultant or contingent.
9. Two Latin terms are applicable. FIRST: Scripture tells us that the Sacred Word of God is to be considered to be true before our experience of it. This is called *a priori* and it is part of biblical faith. Adam and Eve did not grasp this principle! And therefore they experienced the meaning of revelation, *a posteriori*, that is, *after* they had put it to the test! 3:1-7. The same rule still applies.
10. Material Reality is no obstruction to the will of God! Material Reality is not permanent!
11. Implied here is the thought that the Bible stands as the grammar (the rules) for the use of the human language facility! Further, language is a shared conditionality between God and men! It did not "evolve" into existence!
12. Neither is Reality symmetrical; it is, in fact, absolutely asymmetrical! The Spiritual is much more powerful than the Temporal and Material!

Reflecting on Exodus:

What's the Main Point or Generalization this Lesson makes About Reality in this Book of the Bible?

CHANGEPOINTS

I think I need to change my view of reality to match God's in the following areas:

Make a list here of other verses in the book that deal with God's view of reality

1

2

3

4

5

6

7

8

From Exodus

THE STRUCTURE OF REALITY

1. A new king came to power in Egypt. That king did not know the sacred arrangement of reality under Joseph, 1:8.
2. The new potentate, we learn, was an empiricist!
3. Most notably, he operated on what came to be the intuitive comprehension of reality, trying to control the structure of reality, 1:15-17.
4. Eventually the Lord having blessed the biology of the Israelites, who flourished and multiplied in Egypt. The Egyptian government was alarmed. The midwives among the Israelites were instructed to practice infanticide on the male babies (what is now being called post-birth abortion.) The Almighty was not pleased with that sociological policy. The midwives did not comply, 1:21.
5. At that point the causal Reality of God injected Providence into Temporal Reality, 2:3-10.
6. God was quite aware of the then historical conditions, 2:23, 24. The corollary is, the human perception of reality must meet the revealed picture of reality, 3:1-9. "I AM WHO I AM", is the name of the final ultimate reality, 3:14.
7. Many miracles came to bear upon Egypt, 3.:19, 20. And the miracles witness to the Lord's reality, 4:1-13.
8. It is revealed that history traces predetermined paths, 5:1-23. Pharaoh objected: "But Pharaoh said, 'Who is the Lord that I should obey His voice to let Israel go? I do not know the Lord, and besides, I will not let Israel go'", 5:2.
9. However, the power of God, a reality, can be forced into temporal reality, 6:1-13. Such power can also work through chosen human agents, 7:1.
10. Ten plagues, rooted in invisible reality, fell upon Egypt because the leadership did not accept any greater reality, 14-15.
11. And it was that greater reality that could have moderated Pharaoh's behavior!
12. God put sustenance and provision into historical conditions, 15:22-16. More than, that the greater reality put in place the supernatural language manifold, 20.
13. The tabernacle was laid out as a working model of total reality, ch. 25-31. There came a time when even the people of God finally rejected the greater of reality, ch. 32.

Reflecting on Leviticus:

What's the Main Point or Generalization this Lesson makes About Reality in this Book of the Bible?

CHANGEPOINTS

I think I need to change my view of reality to match God's in the following areas:

Make a list here of other verses in the book that deal with God's view of reality

1

2

3

4

5

6

7

8

From LEVITICUS

THE STRUCTURE OF REALITY

1. Throughout the Bible, it becomes noticeable that how one sees reality determines the subsequent pathway of thought, speech and behavior.
2. One may be doctrinaire and yet still hold an insufficient perception of reality! In the indicated biblical text (Leviticus 27) there is what constitutes a hierarchy of "valuation".
3. At the top of the "valuation" hierarchy is that which BELONGS TO THE LORD, v.23, 26, 28, 32.
4. If anything or anyone belongs to the Lord, then that is his/her highest valuation. Intuitive or inherited perceptions of what is real have to correspond to the word of God.
5. A lot of this is incorporated into the TEN COMMANDMENTS: "These are the commandments which the Lord commanded Moses for the sons of Israel at Mount Sinai" 27:34.
6. The Pentateuch consistently teaches that one must see reality, all of it, both the visible and invisible from the Lord's point of view.
7. It becomes significant that the Lord's perception is much advanced beyond the intuitive or empiricist understanding of just what "reality" is and how to represent it.
8. But under no circumstances should one presume that all reality is composed of only that which can be detected by the central nervous system!
9. There is a warning: "… When a man makes a difficult vow, he shall be valued according to your valuation of persons belonging to the Lord", 27:2.
10. The Israelites failed in their perception of reality routinely as difficult circumstances presented themselves! One's view of reality precedes the kind of reasoning in which one indulges! Our responses to "difficult" situations are all tied to ontological issues, like how we perceive "reality"'. The highest "valuation" possible is "to belong to the Lord"! Any other valuation pales in its shadow!

Reflecting on Numbers:

What's the Main Point or Generalization this Lesson makes About Reality in this Book of the Bible?

CHANGEPOINTS

I think I need to change my view of reality to match God's in the following areas:

Make a list here of other verses in the book that deal with God's view of reality

1

2

3

4

5

6

7

8

From Numbers

THE STRUCTURE OF REALITY

1. "Then the Lord spoke to Moses in the wilderness of Sinai, in the tent of meeting. On the first of the second month, in the second year after they had come out of the land of Egypt, saying,", 1:1.
2. There the Israelites were, "… in the wilderness… ". No inherent means of survival available. Yet bored right down into that barren place was "… the tent of meeting… ". And it was from that holy tent that the Lord spoke to the people. From the tent SUPERNATURAL DIRECTIVES were sent ➡ into the minds and hearts of the people. And so the individual Israelites were to function as INSTRUMENTS of the word of God.
3. That provides a kind of summary of the Book of Numbers!
4. THE INVISIBLE REALITY IS DIRECTIVE, and THE VISIBLE REALITY and THE PEOPLE IN IT SERVE AS INSTRUMENTS OF THE SUPERNATURAL WILL.
5. Camp arrangements were strategically established by the Lord, 2:1-34. "Thus the sons of Israel did according to all that the Lord commanded Moses… ", 2:34.
6. The Levites, the priests, were organized in the same manner, 3:1-39. "Duty" was defined from the tent of meeting, 3:25-5:10.
7. Functions of the flesh were addressed by the SUPERNATURAL REALITY and the body was instrumental, 5:11-6:21.
8. The presence of the SUPERNATURAL REALITY demonstrated its determinant actuality: "Now on the day that the tabernacle was erected the cloud covered the tabernacle, the tent of the testimony, and in the evening it was like the appearance of fire over the tabernacle, until morning", 9;15.
9. The sin of complaint (11:10). Then came the revolt of Miriam and Aaron: "Then Miriam and Aaron spoke against Moses because of the Cushite (she was black) woman whom he had married (for he had married a Cushite woman)", 22:1. Neither one sufficiently grasped the true structure of reality!
10. The 40-day reconnaissance mission was mounted and the spies returned to camp, 13:1-14:10. The people of Israel neglected the SUPERNATURAL STRUCTURE OF REALITY and inclined toward the intuitive, empiricist ideology and human experience. Thus they rejected the relation between the two major elements of reality.

11. In their devaluation of the true structure of reality, they resorted to EPISODIC ORGANIZATION. This is the theory of organization by known patterns. Patterns conduce to predictions and outcomes. People can put faith in patterns instead of God! The idea that life is understood in terms of episodic structure. Bad diagnosis leads to unwanted outcomes. But believers are not permitted to fall into that trap. Because THE INVISIBLE REALITY CAN REVERSE ANY SET OF HISTORICAL CONDITIONS. The book of Numbers is, among other things, a corrective of false ideas and false reasoning! 20:1-23. The failure of faith, 22:1-24:9. It is all summed up here: "… Alas, who can live except God has ordained it", 24:23.

Reflecting on Deuteronomy:

What's the Main Point or Generalization this Lesson makes About Reality in this Book of the Bible?

CHANGEPOINTS

I think I need to change my view of reality to match God's in the following areas:

Make a list here of other verses in the book that deal with God's view of reality

1

2

3

4

5

6

7

8

From Deuteronomy

THE STRUCTURE OF REALITY

1. SPIRITUAL REALITY, ACCORDING TO DEUTERONOMY, CAPITALIZES THOSE WHO PURSUE THE WILL OF GOD.
2. Human lived experience is not permitted to overrule the Revealed Word of God, 1:22-26.
3. "The Lord your God who goes before you will Himself fight on your behalf, just as He did for you in Egypt before your eyes", 1:30.
4. Supernatural Reality sets the future, 1:39, 40. "Blessings" are the coinage in this reality, 2:7. And they are a form of SUPERNATURAL CAPITALIZATION.
5. The SUPERNATURAL REALITY allows no compromise on the foundation of Temporal Reality, 7:1-26. Man himself is not sufficiently causal: we need something outside the natural system, 8:17.
6. The TEN COMMA NDMENTS are particles OF THE SUPER SPIRITUAL REALITY, 4:1-49. Under its power, circumstances become non-determinant, 9:1-29.
7. It demands the exclusion of all worldly ideology, 12:1-8. Idolatry as false reality is forbidden, 13:1-18.
8. One shoulders a great deal of personal responsibility, 22-26.
9. Every person stands between the Reality of Curses and Blessings, all emanating from UNSEEN REALITY, 27, 28. CONSEQUENCES unfortunately reign in the affairs of men!
10. A covenant is possible between the 2 parts of reality. An index uniting the Invisible ➡ and the Visible, 29:19, 20.
11. Such ACCOUNTABILITY! Produces a REVOLUTION IN THOUGHT, SPEECH and BEHAVIOR. The world is always trailing behind the SUPERNATURAL REALITY.

Reflecting on Joshua:

What's the Main Point or Generalization this Lesson makes About Reality in this Book of the Bible?

CHANGEPOINTS

I think I need to change my view of reality to match God's in the following areas:

Make a list here of other verses in the book that deal with God's view of reality

1

2

3

4

5

6

7

8

From Joshua

THE STRUCTURE OF REALITY

1. Spiritual REALITY GOVERNS TIME, LIFE and HISTORY. The Lord spoke to Joshua: "Moses My servant is dead; now therefore arise, cross this Jordan, you and all these people, to the land which I am giving to them, to the sons of Israel", 1:2.
2. There are no such articles governing history, often called THE LAWS OF HISTORY.
3. This means that the true context of the life that each of us has is SUPERNATURAL and nontemporal: "This Book of the law shall not depart from your mouth, but you shall meditate on it day and night, so that you may be careful to do according to all that is written in it; For then you will make your way prosperous, and then you will have success", 1:8.
4. And then the promise of God to be an integral part of one's personal history: "Have I not commanded you? Be strong and courageous! Do not tremble or be dismayed, for the Lord your God is with you wherever you go", 1:9.
5. Personal psychology is to be subordinate to the words of God! Depression and hopelessness have no place in such a context of revealed truth!
6. Rahab believed in the finality of the Invisible God: "… He is God in heaven above and on earth beneath", 2:11. No place is isolated; no personal circumstance is independent of SUPERNATURAL REALITY. And that explains her behavior, 1:8-14.
7. Such a configuration of reality requires personal consecration, 3:5. There is another associated reality to be considered: "Behold the ark of the covenant of the Lord of all the earth is crossing over ahead of you into the Jordan", 3:11.
8. The Almighty Invisible Reality struck the psychology of His opponents and their inner resolve melted away, 4, 5. The Lord had invested Himself in the affairs of mortal men and in their weaknesses. He would make the impossible, possible: "Now it came about when Joshua was by Jericho, that he lifted up his eyes and looked, and behold, a man was standing opposite him with his sword drawn in his hand, and Joshua went to him and said to him, are you for us or for our adversaries?". "He said, 'No; rather I indeed come now *as* captain of the host of the Lord.'" 5:13, 14.
9. Without SUPERNATURAL APPROVAL THE OUTCOME IS DISASTER, 7:1-9.

10. What should a believer, who is in over his head, say and do?: "Nevertheless my brethren who went up with me made the heart of the people melt with fear; but I followed the Lord my God fully", 14:8. We go independent of sociology and stick with the word of God and the integrity of the character of God.

The

BIBLE

demands for itself the place of

AGENT

and that we yield our minds to it.

Meme from Representational Research artist Elizabeth Darnell. For information about terms, see the Glossary at RepresentationalResearch.com.

Reflecting on Judges:

What's the Main Point or Generalization this Lesson makes About Reality in this Book of the Bible?

CHANGEPOINTS

I think I need to change my view of reality to match God's in the following areas:

Make a list here of other verses in the book that deal with God's view of reality

1

2

3

4

5

6

7

8

From Judges

THE STRUCTURE OF REALITY

1. In the quandary of uncertainty, we reach out to INVISIBLE REALITY: "Now it came about after the death of Joshua that the sons of Israel inquired of the Lord... ", 1:1.
2. Direction was given, 1:2. The Supreme Reality gave victory in battle to Israel, 1:4-20.
3. But the obedience of the people of God was inconclusive, 1:21-2:3. That half-hearted commitment removed the SPIRITUAL PRECONDITION FOR VICTORY, 2:3. The Lord would not drive out the enemy peoples under those circumstances, where human will supplanted the revealed will of God: "Therefore I also said, 'I will not drive them out before you; but they will become as thorns in your sides and their Gods will be a snare to you'", 2:3.
4. The false reality of idolatry began to rapidly develop its web of lies and deception, 2:1-3:8. REPENTANCE OF ISRAEL CHANGED HISTORICAL CONDITIONS: "When the sons of Israel cried out to the Lord, the Lord raised up a deliverer for the sons of Israel to deliver them... ", 3:9. REPENTANCE is a response to the structure of reality!
5. History is constructed out of the will of God and the power of God, 4:1-5:31.
6. Invisible/Causal Reality is reactive! It reacts to human spiritual negligence, 6:1, 2.
7. Human insufficiency is transformed into supernatural agency, 6:12, "The angel of the Lord appeared to him [Gideon] and said to him, 'The Lord is with you, O valiant warrior'". 7:1-8:35.
8. The will of God functions through even human imperfections: the example of Samson, 13:1-6:31.
9. Unaided human reason is contradictory to the eternal nature of true causal reality: "In those days there was no king in Israel; every man did what was right in his own eyes", 17:6.
10. The battle against wickedness is taxing and necessarily involves all believers. Trouble is inherent in this effort, however, the Lord is directly involved, 19:1-21:25.

Reflecting on Ruth:

What's the Main Point or Generalization this Lesson makes About Reality in this Book of the Bible?

CHANGEPOINTS

I think I need to change my view of reality to match God's in the following areas:

Make a list here of other verses in the book that deal with God's view of reality

1

2

3

4

5

6

7

8

From Ruth

THE STRUCTURE OF REALITY

1. The Book of Ruth presents the idea that REALITY has a SUPERNATURAL AXIS (the invisible part), around which the Temporal part swirls, according to the gravitational pull of the axis.
2. There was a government in place (the judges),1:1. But there was famine in the land of Judah and that, caused by the Axial Power: "… for she (Naomi) had heard in the land of Moab that the Lord had visited His people in giving them food", 1:6.
3. The Lord had imposed a strategic famine, and then He reversed that historical condition.
4. Naomi attributed "kindness" to the Invisible Reality, 1:8. She, as well, attributed all of her distress and loss to that unseen causal force in her personal affairs: "… for it is harder for me than for you, for the hand of the Lord has gone forth against me", 1:13. The Lord had increased and exacerbated her personal anguish! That was quite the case!
5. Naomi did not know the purpose behind her circumstances, all she knew was the most profound anguish! And we are often in that same state of being, so we follow along behind the Lord in complete trust.
6. This is a case of perfect evangelism. Ruth herself, was willing to accept the same Supernatural Axis of personal history. "… Ruth said, 'Do not urge me to leave you or turn back from following you; for where you go, I will go, and where you lodge, I will lodge. Your people shall be my people, and your God, my God. Where you die, I will die, and there I will be buried. This may the Lord do to me, and worse, if anything but death parts you and me", 1:16, 17.
7. Naomi's sense of self had changed dramatically, "… do not call me Naomi; call me Mara, for the Almighty has dealt very bitterly with me", 1:20. "I went out full, but the Lord has brought me back empty. Why do you call me Naomi, since the Lord has witnessed against me and the Almighty has afflicted me", 1:21.
8. Boaz, a wealthy farmer, was one who put his trust in Invisible Reality, "Now behold, Boaz came from Bethlehem and said to the reapers, 'May the Lord be with you.' And they said to him 'May the Lord bless you'", 2:4.
9. Ruth's great devotion to Naomi had become known. "May the Lord reward your work, and your wages be full from the Lord, the God of Israel, under whose wings you have come to seek refuge", 2:12. The divine axis was the source of all wellbeing.

10. Providence was instantly acknowledged by Naomi, in regard to the kindness of Boaz, "… May he be blessed of the Lord who has not withdrawn His kindness to the living and to the dead… ", 2:20.
11. Ruth accorded her behavior in the honorable manner and Boaz respected her even more; God was the witness to this private matter, "Let it not be known that the woman came to the threshing floor", 3:14. A prayer to God was offered for the union of Boaz and Ruth, 4:11. "And the Lord enabled her (Ruth) to conceive, and she gave birth to a son", 4:13.
12. The reach of the SUPERNATURAL AXIS IS LONG and it is deep. Things can turn out very well for those in its orbit! Take heart!! Naomi had the sense that there was a DEEP SPIRITUAL BACKGROUND OR HISTORY TO WHAT HAPPENED TO HER IN LIFE. The Lord plays hardball!

Reflecting on First Samuel:

What's the Main Point or Generalization this Lesson makes About Reality in this Book of the Bible?

CHANGEPOINTS

I think I need to change my view of reality to match God's in the following areas:

Make a list here of other verses in the book that deal with God's view of reality

1

2

3

4

5

6

7

8

From 1 Samuel

THE STRUCTURE OF REALITY

1. The Quickening of that which is dead.
2. A woman from Ramah prayed and for a child, 1:11-20. She was barren. But that which was dead was quickened by the Invisible Reality. Hannah wrote a song of gratitude: "My heart exults in the Lord"… "There is no one holy like the Lord"… "For the Lord is a God of knowledge"… "The bows of the mighty are shattered, but the feeble gird on strength"… "Those who were full hire themselves out for bread, but those who were hungry cease to hunger"… "The Lord kills and makes alive; He brings down to Sheol and raises up"… "He raises the poor from the dust, He brings low, He also exalts"… "He keeps the feet of His godly ones, but the wicked ones are silenced in darkness"… "Those who contend with the Lord will be shattered; against them He will thunder in the heavens"… "The Lord will judge the ends of the earth; and He will give strength to His king, and will exalt the horn of His anointed", 2:1-10.
3. And so His Excellency reverses circumstances for those who trust in Him, the Invisible Reality!
4. The Almighty assigns the particulars of service to chosen people, 3:1-21.
5. Prophecies are leveled for and against certain people, 2:12-36.
6. The Philistine capture of the Ark of the Covenant angered the Lord: "He smote the men of the city (Gath), both young and old, so that tumors broke out on them", 5:9.
7. False gods are demoted and disgraced before the power of the Invisible Reality, 6:4, 5.
8. The Lord God restores the repentant: "… If you return to the Lord with all your heart, remove the foreign gods and the Ashtaroth from among you and direct your hearts to the Lord and serve Him alone; and He will deliver you from the hand of the Philistines", 7:3.
9. Repentance is the key to the restoration of wellbeing! An entire people and individuals are required by the Superconscious Reality to acknowledge His presence, will and power over time, life, history and materiality.
10. The revelation from God is inherently divisive. It separates those who pursue the Invisible Reality and those who look to themselves and this world. The people asked for a king and rejected God, 8:7. Yet Jonathan and his armor bearer sought battle with Philistines, and that with great personal risk! 14:1-23.
11. Relation to the ABSOLUTE STRUCTURE OF REALITY is the key to life on planet earth! Progressivism is meaningless and vacuous!

Reflecting on 2 Samuel:

What's the Main Point or Generalization this Lesson makes About Reality in this Book of the Bible?

CHANGEPOINTS

I think I need to change my view of reality to match God's in the following areas:

Make a list here of other verses in the book that deal with God's view of reality

1

2

3

4

5

6

7

8

From 2 Samuel

THE STRUCTURE OF REALITY

1. "The Lord's anointed", is a station of personal existence. The will of the ABSOLUTE ETERNAL REALITY HAD EXPRESSED HIMSELF. That cannot be violated nor overturned without penalty.
2. David turned to the only mind beyond temporal circumstances: "... David inquired of the Lord", 2:1. David did not turn inward nor to subjectivism but rather to ABSOLUTE OBJECTIVITY. And that Source answered him.
3. It seems that all things temporal are to be referred to the HIGHER ORDER REALITY. "... For the Lord had spoken of David saying, 'By the hand of My servant David I will save My people Israel from the hand of the Philistines and from the hand of all their enemies", 3:18. Human agency put at the disposal of unseen reality.
4. David was devoted to the idea of guilt before God, "I and my kingdom are innocent before the Lord forever of the blood of Amber the son of Ner", 3:28.
5. There was a clash between those who respected the Unseen Reality and those who did not. This is a contemporary clash today. There is no peace between them!
6. The Invisible Almighty is the Prime Adjudicator of human affairs: "... May the Lord repay the evildoer according to his evil", 3:39.
7. THE PRACTICE OF ATTRIBUTION: "The Lord has broken through my enemies before me like the breakthrough of waters". Therefore he named that place Baal-perazim", 5:20. A symbol was generated by the relation of the Unseen ➡ the Seen.
8. The identity and place of the Invisible, "... called by the Name, the very name of the Lord of hosts who is enthroned above the cherubim", 6:2. The veil in which the Lord dwells is quite the part of His being. Not an obstacle to it!
9. The Lord has distinct character properties, "anger", for example, 6:7.
10. Significant blessings flowed from heaven to earth because of one's reverence before the ETERNAL REALITY. A man known as Obed-Edom practiced just such reverence, 6:11, 12.
11. The RELATION BETWEEN THIS TEMPORAL REALITY and that which is unseen had been set from the beginning of time!
12. 7:18-29, demonstrates the exalted nature of the Higher Reality in relation to the lower temporal reality! The earth is a symbol of Supernatural Meaning.

Reflections on this Review:

NOTES

REVIEW

THE STRUCTURE OF REALITY

1. Beginning with the Book of Genesis, a canonical idea takes form from the REVEALED LANGUAGE MANIFOLD. The CANONICAL IDEA: THE TANGIBLE, MEASURABLE PART OF REALITY WAS ALWAYS IMMERSED IN A CLOUD OF SUPERNATURAL CAUSAL HISTORY.
2. According to Genesis chapters 1-3: The temporal material part of reality had that SUPERNATURAL CAUSAL HISTORY as the cause behind, and previous to, the appearance of the visible universe. The narrative regarding Joseph, his life, his works of faith in Egypt were attributed to this DEEP CAUSAL SUPERNATURAL HISTORY BEHIND IT ALL.
3. That generalization came to Joseph with significant emotional effect: "... I am your brother Joseph, whom you sold into Egypt. Now do not be grieved nor angry with yourselves, because you sold me here, for God sent me before you to preserve life", Genesis 45:4, 5. "Now therefore, it was not you who sent me here, but God; and He has made me a father to Pharaoh and lord over all his household and ruler over all the land of Egypt", 45:8.
4. The temporal part of reality is a field developed by this deep SUPERNATURAL CAUSAL HISTORY.
5. There is nothing natural about the emergence of the OBJECTIVE MATERIAL REALITY. It could not have come into being on its own!
6. Moses' life was inexplicable apart from this DEEP SUPERNATURAL CAUSAL HISTORY IN WHICH Moses was born and in which he lived all of his life!
7. He survived long after his birth, even though he was born under a death warrant! He was forced out of Egypt and then years later, suddenly reappeared to confront a notable SUPERPOWER OF ITS DAY, Exodus 2:13-16.
8. The Exodus itself could only have happened by DIVINE INTERVENTION.
9. The chariots of Egypt dramatically appeared, inciting fear and terror! "But Moses said to the people, 'Do not fear! Stand by and see the salvation of the Lord which He will accomplish for you today... ", Exodus 14:13.
10. Rahab perceived the REALITY of this SUPERNATURAL CAUSAL HISTORY ASSOCIATED WITH THE ISRAELITES. Joshua 2:10, 11.
11. In the Book of Ruth, Naomi had grasped the hem of this STRUCTURE WE CHOOSE TO CALL THE SUPERNATURAL CAUSAL HISTORY BEHIND EVENTS. Ruth married Boaz the son of Rahab! Boaz became a voice of

this SUPERNATURAL CAUSAL HISTORY: "May the Lord reward your work, and your wages be full from the Lord, the God of Israel, under whose wings you have come to seek refuge", Ruth 2:12.

12. We can be depressed about our past, perhaps, but look at what has protected us through it all: THE SUPERNATURAL CAUSAL HISTORY. There is eternal purpose in this! Wow!

ADDITIONAL NOTES

Reflecting on 1 Kings:

What's the Main Point or Generalization this Lesson makes About Reality in this Book of the Bible?

CHANGEPOINTS

I think I need to change my view of reality to match God's in the following areas:

Make a list here of other verses in the book that deal with God's view of reality

1

2

3

4

5

6

7

8

From 1 Kings

THE STRUCTURE OF REALITY

1. There was a DEEP REALITY OPERATING IN THE HISTORY OF ISRAEL. One must acknowledge such SUPERNATURAL ENERGY FUNCTIONING IN SPACE, TIME and MATERIALITY. "Keep the charge of the Lord your God, to walk in His ways (SUPERNATURAL WAYS and not RATIONAL WAYS), to keep His statutes, His commandments, His ordinances, And His testimonies, according to what is written in the Law of Moses, that you may succeed in all that you do and wherever you turn", 2:3. The unseen reality drove a wedge between supernatural based reasoning and rational ways of reasoning. What was called "success" was contingent upon the SUPERNATURAL INVISIBLE REALITY and ITS RELATION TO THIS WORLD.
2. Solomon started out very well! He grasped that Israel was not a stereotypical kind of nation. There was a king but the true governance was off-planet! Solomon initially understood that fact.
3. In prayer, Solomon said, "'You have shown great lovingkindness to your servant David my father, according as he walked before You in truth and righteousness and uprightness of heart toward You; and You have reserved for him this great lovingkindness, that You have given him a son to sit on his throne, as it is today," 3:6.
4. Time was involved, biology was involved, but most importantly, INVISIBLE REALITY was involved. Amassing to what we have previously referred to as CONDENSED REALITY (with the Supernatural Reality included it becomes a very "thick" reality!) Solomon sought an immediate and protracted relation to God: "Now, O Lord my God, You have made Your servant king in place of my father David, yet I am but a child; I do not know how to go out or come in. Your servant is in the midst of Your people which You have chosen, a great people who are too many to be numbered or counted. So give Your servant an understanding heart to judge Your people to discern between good and evil. For who is able to judge this great people of Yours", 3:6-9.
5. Solomon was pursuing a SHARED MANNER OF REASONING WITH THE LORD. That was the key to everything in Israel. This request of Solomon was precisely in accordance with the character of God: "It was pleasing in the sight of the Lord that Solomon had asked this thing", 3:10.
6. Clearly, the new king had a prevailing interest, pursuing the approval of God!

7. The basic PRECONDITION for the Israelite people was the approval of the INFINITE REALITY: "But now the Lord my God has given me rest on every side; there is neither adversary nor misfortune", 5:4.
8. Historical Conditions surrounding Israel did not serve as a context, only a setting. The true context was invisible and supernatural.
9. Solomon built the Temple but that structure was dwarfed by the ULTIMATE REALITY! "But will God dwell on the earth? Behold, heaven and the highest heaven cannot contain You, how much less this house which I have built!", 8:27. Prayer is offered upon the bedrock of BIBLICAL REVEALED PLENARY (full/complete) REALITY. "Then hear in heaven Your dwelling place, and forgive and act and render to each according to all his ways, whose heart You know, for You alone know the hearts of all the sons of men", 8:39.
10. The greatest of Reality is there, just over the frontier of The Rational Limits of this world and human perception!

AGENT -> PATIENT

Word of God -> Mind of Man

active passive

Meme from Representational Research artist Elizabeth Darnell. For information about terms, see the Glossary at RepresentationalResearch.com.

Reflecting on 2 Kings:

What's the Main Point or Generalization this Lesson makes About Reality in this Book of the Bible?

CHANGEPOINTS

I think I need to change my view of reality to match God's in the following areas:

Make a list here of other verses in the book that deal with God's view of reality

1

2

3

4

5

6

7

8

From 2 Kings

THE STRUCTURE OF REALITY

1. The SUPERNATURAL REALITY behind all things is incorrigible (uncorrectable). Ahaziah experienced a reversal, 1:2. He wanted to know if he would or could recover from his indisposition. The unseen but nevertheless, ALMIGHTY, sent "the angel of the Lord to the prophet "Elijah the Tishbite saying, 'Arise, go up to meet the messengers of the king of Samaria and say to them, 'Is it because there is no God in Israel that you are going to inquire of Baal-Zebub the god of Ekron?'", 1:3. And that was a rhetorical question.
2. "Now therefore thus says the Lord, 'You shall not come down from the bed where you have gone up, but you shall surely die', then Elijah departed,'". So THE GREATER REALITY DETERMINED THAT NOT ONLY WOULD HE NOT SURVIVE, BUT THAT HE COULD NOT RECOVER. 1:4.
3. Ahaziah correctly surmised that it was the prophet Elijah (who spoke for the Invisible) with whom they met, 1:6-8.
4. The king of Samaria issued orders to arrest and detain Elijah, 1:9. 50 soldiers and a captain were dispatched to execute the warrant. But Elijah waited for them on a hill. The captain expected that 50 men would be enough to do the job. Elijah said to the captain, "'... If I am a man of God, let fire come down from heaven and consume you and your fifty.' Then fire came down from heaven and consumed him and his fifty", 1:10.
5. And that was that! A second unit of 50 men and their captain came, being dispatched to arrest Elijah. Fire from heaven consumed them alive! 1:11, 12. It's all here!
6. A third cohort of 50 came to get Elijah. But this time, the captain had thought it through on supernatural terms. "When the third captain of fifty went up, he came and bowed down on his knees before Elijah, and begged him and said to him, 'O man of God, please let my life and the lives of these fifty servants of yours be precious in your sight. The angel of the Lord said to Elijah, 'Go down with him; do not be afraid of him", 1:13-15.
7. The king of Samaria sent men to get Elijah and shut him up. The government can say, "O man of God, the king says, 'Come down'", 1:9, 11. But one must decide with whom one stands! The last captain had understood that the king had authority but that there is a Higher Reality than the worldly government with its powers of censure and arrest.
8. The last captain realized he had to have a higher loyalty and he complied!

9. This is the position of believers in the contemporary! We are charged with a high degree of responsibility to that HIGHER ORDER OF REALITY. No compromise is permitted! The wise captain acknowledged that it was a matter of power. And therefore, the situation was greatly SUPERNATURAL. There was nothing natural about it!
10. Some believers, when confronted by the clinical, the political, or perhaps the financial, think that God is absent from such circumstances, however, that is a great mistake. God was with the Tishbite and that was quite sufficient!
11. One cannot silence nor isolate nor censure any chosen vessel of HIGHER ABSOLUTE REALITY with any expectation of success!
12. He, that is, the Divine Personage is INCORRIGIBLE! That one cannot be corrected by mere men!

AGENT -> PATIENT

Word of God -> Mind of Man

Meme from Representational Research artist Elizabeth Darnell. For information about terms, see the Glossary at RepresentationalResearch.com.

Reflecting on 1 Chronicles:

What's the Main Point or Generalization this Lesson makes About Reality in this Book of the Bible?

CHANGEPOINTS

I think I need to change my view of reality to match God's in the following areas:

Make a list here of other verses in the book that deal with God's view of reality

1

2

3

4

5

6

7

8

From 1 Chronicles

THE STRUCTURE OF REALITY

1. What we have in this book is supernatural perception of time. And nobody has a sufficient definition, let alone understanding of what time is.
2. Routinely time is defined by our intuition of it! It appears to be behaving like a speeding bullet moving off into the distance with all of us left behind.
3. However, the genealogy in this text is certainly suggestive of the opposite. It suggests that the passage of time represented by the persons named in the list was and is constantly CONTRACTING back upon the will, the word and the power of God!
4. "Now Jabez called on the God of Israel, saying, 'Oh that You would bless me indeed and enlarge my border, and that Your hand might be with me, and that you would keep me from harm that it may not pain me!' And God granted him what he requested", 4:10.
5. Jabez wanted historical conditions to be forced to CONTRACT UPON the Invisible causal reality!
6. This force of Contraction is not intuitive nor psychological. Rather it is revealed through the power of the word of God! It reflects precisely how the Almighty relates to the temporal order in which men live and move!
7. Because of CONTRACTION we learn that PRAYER ➡ and TRUST ARE TIGHTLY WOUND TOGETHER AS ONE PIECE.
8. Of the tribe of Reuben, they consisted of "… valiant men, men who bore shield and sword and shot with bow and were skillful in battle, were 44,760 who went to war. They made war against the Hagrites, Jetur, Naphish and Nidab. They were helped against them, and the Hagrites and all who were with them were given into their hand; for they cried out to God in the battle, and He answered their prayers because they trusted in Him", 5:18-20.
9. The battle began and they were losing! But they PRAYED IN COMPLETE TRUST and the Invisible Reality CONTRACTED THE BATTLE in favor of Reuben!
10. The tribe of Reuben had to look beyond TEMPORAL REALITY FOR SUCCESS. Things, no matter how hopeless they appear, can still be forced into SUPERNATURAL CONTRACTION. It is never too late! Perhaps we should seriously consider this STRUCTURE OF REALITY.
11. CONTRACTION CAN BE A BLESSING TO SOME and A DANGER TO OTHERS: "… And Judah was carried away into exile to Babylon for their unfaithfulness", 9:1. Things are not as they appear!

Reflecting on 2 Chronicles:

What's the Main Point or Generalization this Lesson makes About Reality in this Book of the Bible?

CHANGEPOINTS

I think I need to change my view of reality to match God's in the following areas:

Make a list here of other verses in the book that deal with God's view of reality

1

2

3

4

5

6

7

8

From 2 Chronicles

THE STRUCTURE OF REALITY

1. The Invisible Reality has a function; it is a PRESENCE. In fact, the Invisible Reality serves as the power behind the throne.
2. "Now Solomon the son of David established himself securely over his kingdom, and the Lord his God was with him and exalted him greatly", 1:1.
3. The absolute Precondition for national wellbeing was the power of Invisible Reality expressing itself on behalf of those who trust in the Presence.
4. The Presence is not localized but it is locally symbolized. In this case it was the "tent of meeting", set up at Gibeon, 1:3. This symbol of Invisible Reality was able to focus the interest of Solomon. He didn't worship the symbol, rather he worshiped the unseen God behind it!
5. "Solomon went up there before the Lord to the bronze altar which was at the tent of meeting, and offered a thousand burnt offerings on it", 1:6. Then something remarkable transpired: "In that night God appeared to Solomon and said to him, 'Ask what I shall give you?", 1:7. Solomon acknowledged the TRUE STRUCTURE OF REALITY, "Give me now wisdom and knowledge, that I may go out and come in before this people, for who can rule this great people of Yours?" 1:10.
6. The new king believed in and trusted the MOST ACTIVE ELEMENT OF REALITY, the Invisible part! Solomon initially believed in the DIRECT RELATION BETWEEN THE INVISIBLE ➡ and VISIBLE PARTS OF REALITY. In other words, REALITY IS A UNITY.
7. It appears that the contemporary world has lost the appreciation of this supernatural unity!
8. Much to Solomon's credit, he grasped that SUPERNATURAL WISDOM (ideas) was necessary for a healthy collective. And so the king was prepared to push SUPERNATURAL REASONING (founded upon revelation) into the temporal circumstances of the realm!
9. "Wisdom and knowledge have been granted to you… ", 1:12.
10. "So Solomon went from the high place which was at Gibeon, from the tent of meeting, to Jerusalem, and he reigned over Israel", 1:13.
11. This tells us that Solomon was committed to PUSHING SUPERNATURAL REVEALED INTELLIGENCE INTO TEMPORAL REALITY. Wow! How can we improve on that? Without it a dimension of reality is missing!

Reflecting on Ezra:

What's the Main Point or Generalization this Lesson makes About Reality in this Book of the Bible?

CHANGEPOINTS

I think I need to change my view of reality to match God's in the following areas:

Make a list here of other verses in the book that deal with God's view of reality

1

2

3

4

5

6

7

8

From Ezra

THE STRUCTURE OF REALITY.

1. The SUPERNATURAL CAUSAL HISTORY WAS AT WORK GIVING ENFORCED SHAPE TO EVENTS, circumstances and historical conditions!
2. "Now in the first year of Cyrus king of Persia, in order to fulfill the word of the Lord by the mouth of Jeremiah, the Lord stirred up the spirit of Cyrus king of Persia, so that he sent a proclamation throughout all his kingdom, and also put it in writing, saying: 'Thus says Cyrus king of Persia, the Lord God of heaven, has given me all the kingdoms of the earth and He has appointed me to build Him a house in Jerusalem, which is in Judah'", 1:1, 2.
3. Those ideas did not originate on earth, nor in the consciousness of Cyrus! Those thoughts began in the mind of God and in eternity! Men usually take for granted that history is transparent to the observer. But that is a big mistake!
4. The TEMPORAL ELEMENT OF REALITY is not a closed system! Quite to the reverse everything in it is open to the INVISIBLE REALITY.
5. Not even Cyrus the powerful potentate of Persia was immune to the ABSOLUTE REALITY governing the future.
6. Ezra wants the reader to know that time is not merely a product of PROCESS, indeed time and the events in it are the result of a SUPER and SUPERIOR CONSCIOUSNESS. That in itself is an overwhelming thought!
7. "Then the heads of fathers' households of Judah and Benjamin and the priests and the Levite's arose, even everyone in whose spirit God had stirred to go up and rebuild the house of the Lord which is in Jerusalem", 1:5.
8. The Invisible Reality was close enough to directly affect the reasoning and behavior of individuals and collectives. The Invisible Element of Reality was in the driver's seat. HISTORY CAN BE TURNED INTO THE VEHICLE FOR THE PURPOSE OF GOD. It is not a free-range chicken! This must apply to one's personal history as well! Perhaps we could/should think in terms of CONDENSED HISTORY. A history thick with substance and resilient to opposition. Things do not just happen! History is resultant; it is the outcome of the relation between the two large distinct elements of Reality, the INVISIBLE and the VISIBLE.
9. Each of us is immersed in a STRUCTURE THAT IS INESCAPABLE and IRREDUCIBLE, a very CONDENSED STRUCTURE. The wise worshiped the INVISIBLE CAUSAL REALITY. The Lord demonstrated on many occasions through chosen symbols (visual) yet the Almighty conserved His invisibility! But invisibility requires faith in one ORDER OF REALITY OVER THE OTHER.

Reflecting on Nehemiah:

What's the Main Point or Generalization this Lesson makes About Reality in this Book of the Bible?

CHANGEPOINTS

I think I need to change my view of reality to match God's in the following areas:

Make a list here of other verses in the book that deal with God's view of reality

1

2

3

4

5

6

7

8

From Nehemiah

THE STRUCTURE OF REALITY

1. Nehemiah was at great distance from Jerusalem in Susa in Persia,1:1. Hanani brought word to Nehemiah about the dismal conditions, 1:2, 3.
2. Nehemiah turned to INVISIBLE REALITY for help and guidance. "I said, I beseech You, O Lord God of heaven, the great and awesome God, who preserves the covenant and lovingkindness for those who love Him and keep His commandments", 1:5.
3. Nehemiah knew, he believed, that INVISIBLE REALITY was the axis of the entire set of historical conditions in Jerusalem.
4. "O Lord, I beseech You. May Your ear be attentive to the prayer of Your servant and the prayer of Your servants who delight to revere Your name, and make Your servant successful today and grant him compassion before this man", 1:11. Nehemiah referred to the king!
5. Nehemiah, to the king, appeared to be disturbed, 2:2. He asked the king for time off, letters of transit, lumber. It was all granted to Nehemiah by the great king! Because "... the good hand of my God was on me", 2:8. An UNSEEN REALITY was structuring events and syntax!
6. Nehemiah arrived in Jerusalem and among his enemies, 2:11. He had a purpose but, he "... did not tell anyone what my God was putting into my mind to do for Jerusalem... ", 2:12 Nehemiah was overpowered by SUPERNATURAL IDEAS, irresistible and driving him onward! The SUPERNATURAL CAUSAL and INVISIBLE REALITY is not mute! He prayed for guidance and He got it! The INDEX BETWEEN THE PARTS OF REALITY IS GREATER THAN TIME and HISTORICAL CONDITIONS. Nor could it be ignored! Should you or I be put into such a state of communication with the Invisible Reality we must follow it to its terminus! That is our duty, privilege and honor!
7. Nehemiah's commitment was total and complete! He did not waver, nor temporize, rather, he immediately engaged with the mission! He predicated success upon one foundation: "I told them how the hand of my God had been favorable to me and also about the king's words which he had spoken to me... ", 2:18. God is not neutral, blind nor disinterested! His named enemies (Sanballat, Tobiah, Geshem) mocked him, 2:19.
8. Nevertheless, Nehemiah remained resolute and faithful! "... The God of heaven will give us success; therefore we His servants will arise and build, but you have no portion, right or memorial in Jerusalem", 2:20.

9. THAT IS OUR EXACT SAME MOTIVE. If and or when the INVISIBLE REALITY CALLS OUT TO US, WE MUST ARISE, GET TO IT and BE RESOLUTE. NO TURNING BACK. NOT WORRYING ABOUT OUTCOMES. BUT LAY HOLD OF THE MISSION, THE ETERNAL DIRECTIVE WITHOUT DELAY. GOD BE WITH YOU ALL!

Reflecting on Esther:

What's the Main Point or Generalization this Lesson makes About Reality in this Book of the Bible?

CHANGEPOINTS

I think I need to change my view of reality to match God's in the following areas:

Make a list here of other verses in the book that deal with God's view of reality

1

2

3

4

5

6

7

8

From Esther

THE STRUCTURE OF REALITY

1. Esther came into public consciousness in an already boiling pressure cooker!
2. Threats were increasing to measurable magnitudes, 3:1-15. Queen Vasthi was demoted, 1:10-22.
3. Eventually, Esther became queen of Persia. 2:17-20.
4. Haman was ratcheting up persecution of the Jews, 3:1-15.
5. Esther had to make an apparently dangerous decision. It was time to stand up for her people or cave to obvious and immediate fear. Mordecai, her uncle, said to her, "Do not imagine that you in the King's palace can escape any more than all the Jews. For if you remain silent at this time, relief and deliverance will arise for the Jews from another place and you and your father's house will perish. And who knows whether you have not attained royalty for such a time as this?" 4:13
6. Mordecai called Esther to a transcendent duty! And there were tangible risks and uncertainty, 4:11.
7. So Esther prepares herself for the strategic moment, 4:15-17. This is not uncommon, is it? The times come when we have to put up or shut up! With the fears and risks sticking in our throats! Mordecai warned Esther, that perhaps PROVIDENCE WAS AT WORK IN ALL THE COMPLEXITY OF THE SITUATION and TO RUN THE RISK WITH COURAGE and RESOLUTION. And she did! 5:1-8.
8. The Queen sticks her neck out and the Jews are delivered, 7:1-6; 9:1-19.
9. The memorial of "Purim" was instituted. A memorial of courage, hope, defeated fears and final deliverance! Queen Esther offers a symbol of all that is good, right and true about faith! Her example of spiritual greatness can help us as we confront what must be done under the battle flag of the ALMIGHTY. It's time to saddle up, I think!

Reflecting on Job:

What's the Main Point or Generalization this Lesson makes About Reality in this Book of the Bible?

CHANGEPOINTS

I think I need to change my view of reality to match God's in the following areas:

Make a list here of other verses in the book that deal with God's view of reality

1

2

3

4

5

6

7

8

From Job

THE STRUCTURE OF REALITY

1. The faith of Job was dependent upon just how that man comprehended the STRUCTURE OF REALITY.
2. HISTORICAL MATERIALISM IS ONE OF THE PRINCIPLES OF MARXISM. That principle stipulates that subsequent human history is determined by material conditions and not by ideas, even what are called "great ideas".
3. "Satan" is a factor in the STRUCTURE OF REALITY. He is active and very interested in human history, 1:7. Satan knows the God of the Bible; he further knows that God is determinant in the affairs of men! "Have You not made a hedge about him and his house and all that he has, on every side?… ", 1:10.
4. The INVISIBLE REALITY was invested in a man and his family in time, space and materiality!
5. Satan, however, was a materialist and thought that men were equally materialistic by nature. "But put forth Your hand now and touch all that he has; he will surely curse You to Your face", 1:11.
6. HISTORICAL MATERIALISM is not just unspiritual, it is anti-spiritual! One concludes, therefore, that MARXISM IS SATANIC FROM THE BIBLE'S POINT OF VIEW.
7. Job understood that the PRECONDITIONS for his success were anything but MATERIALISTIC, those PRECONDITIONS WERE ALL and ONLY SPIRITUAL.
8. Job had to contend with the Lord's INVISIBILITY; and the seeming uncertainties that come with it! Faith was his only course: "The pillars of heaven tremble and are amazed at His rebuke. He quieted the sea with His power, and by His understanding He shattered Rahab. By His breath the heavens are cleared; His hand has pierced the fleeing serpent. Behold, these are the fringes of His ways; and how faint a word we hear of Him! But His mighty thunder, who can understand?", 26:11-14.
9. The human race is suspended in the INVISIBLE REALITY and it is He who whispers to us! Only those of faith can hear it!
10. Job's faith surrendered to no RATIONAL LIMITS. "For as long as life is in me, and the breath of God is in my nostrils, my lips will certainly not speak unjustly, nor will my tongue mutter deceit", 27:3, 4. His faith rested upon the REVEALED STRUCTURE OF REALITY. The Marxists are dead wrong, godless and satanic!

Reflecting on the Psalms:

What's the Main Point or Generalization this Lesson makes About Reality in this Book of the Bible?

CHANGEPOINTS

I think I need to change my view of reality to match God's in the following areas:

Make a list here of other verses in the book that deal with God's view of reality

1

2

3

4

5

6

7

8

From the Psalms

THE STRUCTURE OF REALITY

1. The Psalms covers a lot of territory, but without being too reductive, one can say that the Psalms are frequently found to be appeals made by men in time, materiality and circumstance to a HIGHER ORDER REALITY. *Appeal* to God for help, deliverance and mercy.
2. From this, one may conclude that we all live in what may be called an APPELLATE UNIVERSE.
3. Meditation on the word of God is a fixture in this kind of universe; one responsive to HIGHER ORDER REALITY. "… blessed is the man… (whose) delight is in the law of the Lord, and in His law he meditates day and night", 1:1, 2.
4. One does not cave in to human experience. "Many are saying of my soul, 'There is no deliverance for him in God'", 3:2.
5. David believed in the APPELLATE UNIVERSE: "Answer me when I call, O God of my righteousness! You have relieved me in my distress; be gracious to me and hear my prayer" 4:1.
6. There is no sign of hopelessness in the APPELLATE UNIVERSE. "O Lord my God, in You I have taken refuge; save me from all those who pursue me, and deliver me", 7:1.
7. There is a court of HIGHER APPEAL: "I will give thanks to the Lord with all my heart; I will tell of Your wonders. I will be glad and exult in You; I will sing praise to Your name, O Most High", 9:1, 2.
8. Throughout the Psalms, there are repeated appeals to the HIGHER ORDER REALITY. This is the ARRANGEMENT established by God and it runs between the INVISIBLE ONE ➡ and men in time, space and materiality! It is a factor in biblical faith! Men are built to "look up", to something larger, greater and exalted. And that challenges the supposed primacy of empiricism, materialism, naturalism and human lived experience! There is more to reality than what there appears to be!
9. Spiritual people all have the same thing in common: they seek something that they cannot see but believe that is there, nonetheless!
10. The behavior of such believers is determined by their comprehension of REALITY. "How blessed are those whose way is blameless, who walk in the law of the Lord… . who observe His testimonies, who seek Him with all their heart", 119:1, 2. And they hold to the same structure of life: "I long for Your salvation, O Lord, and Your Law is my delight", 119:174.

Reflecting on the Proverbs:

What's the Main Point or Generalization this Lesson makes About Reality in this Book of the Bible?

CHANGEPOINTS

I think I need to change my view of reality to match God's in the following areas:

Make a list here of other verses in the book that deal with God's view of reality

1

2

3

4

5

6

7

8

From Proverbs

THE STRUCTURE OF REALITY

1. There is a hierarchy of knowledge and of knowing (called epistemology). Knowledge about the TEMPORAL REALITY has its importance but it is eclipsed by another range of knowing: "… then you will discern the fear of the Lord and discover the knowledge of God", 2:6. Such knowledge feeds the spiritual part of man, 2:10.
2. THERE IS A PERSISTENT MESSAGE IN THE BIBLE: EVERY PART OF CREATED REALITY HAS A SPIRITUAL SUBSTRATE (the underlying causal reality or substance). "So You will find favor and good repute in the sight of God and man", 3:4, 5. This SPIRITUAL SUBSTRATE being the case present, then, "Trust in the Lord with all your heart and do not lean on your own understanding", 3:5.
3. Rather, do this in acknowledgement of the GRAND SPIRITUAL SUBSTRATE; "in all your ways acknowledge Him, and He will make your paths straight. Do not be wise in your own eyes; fear the Lord and turn away from evil", 3:6.
4. However, there can be a severe contradiction between one's will and the SPIRITUAL SUBSTRATE.
5. It is upon this foundation, therefore, that the profile of VALID INSTRUCTION IS DETERMINED, 5:12-13.
6. The teaching from the SPIRITUAL SUBSTRATE FORCES DISTINCTIONS IN THOUGHT, SPEECH and BEHAVIOR, "The fear of the Lord is to hate evil; pride and arrogance and the evil way and the perverted mouth, I hate. Counsel is mine and sound wisdom; I am understanding, Power is mine", 8:13, 14.
7. Wisdom is not inherent in man, any man, or any group of men. It has a SUPERNATURAL ORIGIN and it is revealed, not evolved. "The fear of the Lord is the beginning of wisdom, and the knowledge of the Holy One is understanding, 9:10. The fear of God is essential because it holds the mind and the body in its uncompromising embrace!
8. What we now call TRANSPARENCY, is a myth! Unless it is rooted in the revelation from God. "A false balance is an abomination to the Lord, but a just weight is His delight", 11:1.
9. THE INVISIBLE REALITY functions as the SPIRITUAL SUBSTRATE OF ALL THINGS. We are not alone here! The universe of created things does not immediately nor thoroughly correspond to human wisdom (COVID-19 for example).

10. THE INVISIBLE REALITY is not like men, His ways are not dictated by anything historical nor temporal; "The refining pot is for silver and the furnace for gold, but the Lord tests hearts", 17:3. That must be our great concern.

Reflecting on Ecclesiastes:

What's the Main Point or Generalization this Lesson makes About Reality in this Book of the Bible?

CHANGEPOINTS

I think I need to change my view of reality to match God's in the following areas:

Make a list here of other verses in the book that deal with God's view of reality

1

2

3

4

5

6

7

8

From Ecclesiastes

THE STRUCTURE OF REALITY.

1. "A generation goes and another generation comes", 1:4.
2. The author gives a kind of warning: WITHIN TOUCHABLE REALITY, men are only temporary! Not one can stay here with any degree of permanence. All things and everyone is in a STATE OF FLUX! 1:5. PROGRESS is only partially manageable, 1:7.
3. There is uncertainty as to whether one can ever grab a complete sense of fulfillment here in this world! 1:8-11.
4. Men find it impossible to transcend the STRUCTURE OF THIS PART OF REALITY, 1:13-18.
5. The pursuit of experience, accumulation of wealth, and even accomplishments of a material/technical kind do not cover one's interest in the sense of "profit", 2:1-11.
6. A man's identity and contributions are lost in the flux of time, 2:13-17. One man generates great things and then, one follows who reverses it all! 2:18-23. And so ➡ "There is nothing better for a man than to eat and drink and tell himself that his labor is good. This also I have seen that it is from the hand of God", 2:24.
7. The movement of time is marked by significant personal events, 3:1-10. That is how we keep track of it.
8. THE TEMPORAL ORDER IS DIRECTLY ACCOUNTABLE TO THE HIGHER ORDER INVISIBLE REALITY, 3:11-22.
9. We are all SUSPENDED IN THE REALITY OF GOD: "Guard your steps as you go to the house of God and draw near to listen rather than to offer the sacrifice of fools; for they do not know they are doing evil. Do not be hasty in word or impulsive in thought to bring up a matter in the presence of God. For God is in heaven and you are on the earth: therefore let your words be few", 5:1, 2.
10. On the earth, some things that are final: "Consider the work of God, for who is able to straighten what He has bent?", 7:13. The Lord's determinations cannot be overruled by men in time! There is no symmetry between the INVISIBLE ➡ and the VISIBLE.

Reflecting on Isaiah:

What's the Main Point or Generalization this Lesson makes About Reality in this Book of the Bible?

CHANGEPOINTS

I think I need to change my view of reality to match God's in the following areas:

Make a list here of other verses in the book that deal with God's view of reality

1 ______________________

2 ______________________

3 ______________________

4 ______________________

5 ______________________

6 ______________________

7 ______________________

8 ______________________

From Isaiah

THE STRUCTURE OF REALITY

1. The temporal/material universe was conceived by the INVISIBLE GOD as a moral one, "Alas, sinful nation, people weighed down with iniquity, offspring of evildoers, sons who act corruptly! They have abandoned the Lord, they have despised the Holy One of Israel, they have turned away from Him", 1:4.
2. Isaiah sees an arrangement wherein the VISIBLE PART OF REALITY IS SUBMERGED WITHIN THE EMBRACE OF THE INVISIBLE, "… I have had enough of burnt offerings of rams and the fat of fed cattle; and I take no pleasure in the blood of bulls, lambs or goats. When you come to appear before Me, who requires of you this trampling of My courts?", 1:11, 12.
3. There is a linguistic relation between the two parts of reality: "Come now, let us reason together… ", 1:18.
4. INVISIBLE REALITY sits in judgment upon those in time: "Their land had also been filled with idols; they worship the work of their hands, that which their fingers have made", 2:8.
5. Rebellion has only one outcome: "For the Lord of hosts will have a day of reckoning against everyone who is proud and lofty and against everyone who is lifted up, that he may be abased", 2:12.
6. INVISIBLE REALITY reigns supreme over all temporality: " In the year of King Uzziah's death I saw the Lord sitting on a throne, lofty and exalted, with the train of His robe filling the temple", 6:1. The Lord is not defeated! Quite the opposite: He is fully in command of His creation! He is not unattended: "Seraphim stood above Him, each having six wings: with two He covered his face, and with two he covered his feet, and with two he flew", 6:2.
7. The Lord is attended by mobile and powerful angels, geared to exercise the will of God in time and among men!
8. And all men will awaken to His supernatural presence, "And the foundations of the thresholds trembled at the voice of him who called out, while the temple was filled with smoke. Then I said, 'Woe is me, for I am ruined! Because I am a man of unclean lips; and I live among a people of unclean lips, for my eyes have seen the King, the Lord of hosts'. Then one of the seraphim flew to me with burning coal in his hand, which he had taken from the altar with tongs. He touched my

mouth with it and said, 'Behold, this has touched your lips; and your iniquity is taken away and your sin is forgiven'", 6:4-7.

9. The people of God do not adapt to the behavior of the world! Believers are cleansed from unclean lips and we respect that differential!
10. Believers dwell within the REVEALED STRUCTURE OF REALITY and they preach it and defend its integrity!

Reflecting on Jeremiah:

What's the Main Point or Generalization this Lesson makes About Reality in this Book of the Bible?

CHANGEPOINTS

I think I need to change my view of reality to match God's in the following areas:

Make a list here of other verses in the book that deal with God's view of reality

1

2

3

4

5

6

7

8

From Jeremiah

THE STRUCTURE OF REALITY

1. As the prophet writes, the idea becomes more sustainable, that God must be treated as an OBJECTIVE REALITY. The German philosopher, Friedrich Nietzsche, had insisted that God is nothing more than a product of human imagination!
2. In other words, God has become irrelevant! Outmoded and superfluous! Jeremiah might have even considered the idea himself.
3. But then the Lord came quite close: "Before I formed you in the womb I knew you, and before you were born I consecrated you; I have appointed you a prophet to the nations", 1:5.
4. The infidel philosopher had insisted that God, as a causal personality, was effectively dead. Not literally, but since many Europeans refused to live according to His requirements, then God was in all practical ways dead!
5. Nietzsche was attacking what was at the time the traditional STRUCTURE OF REALITY. That TRADITIONAL STRUCTURE maintained that there was a UNITY between GOD ➡ and CAUSATION, chapters 42, 44.
6. But Jeremiah reports that the practice of IDOLATRY HAD BROKEN THAT UNITY BETWEEN GOD and CAUSATION. That meant that the people of the Lord could go after CAUSATION and not go after the INVISIBLE REALITY.
7. In effect, it was thought that any CAUSAL CONNECTION BETWEEN GOD and the TEMPORAL ORDER was abrogated! It is at that point that God becomes perceived as irrelevant to mankind, chapter 44.
8. This is the reason why Jeremiah was sent to prophesy. "I will pronounce My judgments on them concerning all their wickedness, whereby they have forsaken Me and have offered sacrifices to other gods, and worshipped the works of their own hands", 1:16.
9. The relation between God ➡ and CAUSATION is of superior importance to those who chafe under the Lord's limitations on personal behavior!
10. The genius of IDOLATRY is its agenda of separating God from CAUSATION, rendering Him impotent, it is supposed, in our reasoning! This is precisely that which is behind so many contemporary WORLD IDEOLOGIES. MARXISM and SOCIALISM among them. The phenomenon of HUMAN LANGUAGE IS OPERATING AT THE DEEPEST LEVELS IN ALL OF THIS!

Reflecting on Lamentations:

What's the Main Point or Generalization this Lesson makes About Reality in this Book of the Bible?

CHANGEPOINTS

I think I need to change my view of reality to match God's in the following areas:

Make a list here of other verses in the book that deal with God's view of reality

1

2

3

4

5

6

7

8

From Lamentations

THE STRUCTURE OF REALITY

1. INVISIBLE REALITY IS INDEXED (LINKED, tethered together, or bridged) to VISIBLE REALITY. This INDEX is also part of the STRUCTURE OF REALITY.
2. Regardless of what people may "sense", intuit or suppose, not one of us is ever independent of the INVISIBLE part of reality. In fact, each one of us is morally, spiritually accountable to it!
3. "Her adversaries have become her masters, her enemies prosper; for the Lord has caused her grief because of the multitude of her transgressions; her little ones have gone away as captives before the adversary", 1:5.
4. TWO THINGS: (1) CAUSATION runs unidirectionally from INVISIBLE ➡ to VISIBLE. This is noncommutative (moves in one direction only) (2) Necessarily, then, that arrangement between the two is preexistent to TEMPORAL ANYTHING.
5. THEREFORE, THEN, ONE MUST TAKE THE STRUCTURE OF REALITY AS IT COMES and NOT AS WE SUPPOSE IT TO BE.
6. We are all dependent upon that which is independent of us! "All her people groan seeking bread; they have given their precious things for food to restore their lives themselves. See, O Lord, and look, for I am despised", 1:11.
7. The gravity of this INDEX IS SUPERNATURAL: "The yoke of my transgressions is bound; By His hand they are knit together. They have come upon my neck; He has made my strength fail. The Lord has given me into the hands of those against whom I am not able to stand", 1:14.
8. This means that NATURAL ANYTHING can be thoroughly neutralized. We cannot count on any NATURAL FORCE TO SAVE US. Think ENVIRONMENTALISM, CLIMATOLOGY, etc.
9. Not the feelings of the author, not the result of psychologization of external conditions, but, the imposition of INVISIBLE REALITY: "See, O Lord, for I am in distress; my spirit is greatly troubled; my heart is overturned within me, for I have been very rebellious. In the street the sword slays; in the house it is like death", 1:20.
10. Due to some forms of HUMAN BEHAVIOR, consequences appear. For instance, a people can be covered, as if like a cloud, and that by the ANGER OF GOD, 2:1. In such a case, no political, economic nor policy changes will work! Those kinds of things do not encompass the understanding of the CASE PRESENT. And that comprehension is vital to

us, within the BIBLICAL STRUCTURE OF REALITY. The end will be supernatural and grave: "How lonely sits the city That *once* had many people! She has become like a widow *Who was once* great among the nations! *She who was* a princess among the provinces Has become a forced laborer!" 1:1

AGENT -> PATIENT

relationship

Meme from Representational Research artist Elizabeth Darnell. For information about terms, see the Glossary at RepresentationalResearch.com.

Reflections on this Generalization:

NOTES

GENERALIZATION

THE STRUCTURE OF REALITY

1. Human behavior is more than FORM!
2. We could think in terms of ISOMORPHIC BEHAVIORAL SYSTEMS. The term isomorphic simply means 2 things with "the same shape".
3. This means that behavior is a form of CAUSE ➡ to EFFECT. It all starts with the IDEA. But then the idea, something abstract, takes on tangible, noticeable shape or presence! And that shape is exactly that of the IDEA preceding it.
4. There is a CAUSAL RELATION BETWEEN IDEAS and FORMS. IDEAS PRECEDE THE FORM OF THE BEHAVIOR.
5. In spite of the fact that IDEAS ARE ABSTRACT, they still possess a CAUSAL AGENCY.
6. Children go to school, spending their days in absorbing or at least being exposed to various IDEAS that can directly affect BEHAVIORAL FORMS.
7. In the contemporary, we hear of the actions of BLACK LIVES MATTER and ANTIFA. Burning cities, rampaging spoliation of the property of others! All of those BEHAVIORAL FORMS were preceded by IDEAS.
8. Therefore, there is a significant importance associated with the IDEAS behind those FORMS OF BEHAVIOR.
9. The recent foolishness directly related to GENDER REASSIGNMENT CAN BE UNDERSTOOD IN TERMS OF BEHAVIORAL SYSTEMS. What are the IDEAS PRECEDING THE BEHAVIORAL FORMS OF SUPPOSED GENDER TRANSITIONS? Crime, in general, begins with wrong and ultimately destructive IDEAS destined to take on BEHAVIORAL FORMS. The Book of Lamentations is ahead of the game!
10. "Their heart cried out to the Lord, O wall of the daughter of Zion, let your tears run down like a river day and night; give yourself no relief, let your eyes have no rest", 2:18.
11. The central axis of BEHAVIOR ARE the IDEAS and the human will to act upon them!
12. Changing one's ideas is to change one's BEHAVIOR. Hear the words of the prophet: "Remember my affliction and my wandering, the wormwood and bitterness. Surely my soul remembers and is bowed down within me. This I recall to my mind, therefore I have hope", 3:19-21. We thank the Lord for this wisdom! The proper reaction to behavioral systems grows out of the STRUCTURE OF REALITY as biblically represented!

Reflections on this Generalization:

NOTES

GENERALIZATION

THE STRUCTURE OF REALITY.

1. There is a linguistic phenomenon that we might refer to as SYNTHETIC WISDOM. The first instance of this we find in Genesis 3.
2. The contemporary professional practice of journalism is no longer worthy of the name! They persistently respond to logical facts and historical conditions by SYNTHETIC WISDOM. This is a "wisdom" SYNTHESIZED FROM HUMAN WILL, DISHONESTY, and THE MANEUVER OF DISTORTION. IDEOLOGY is a large factor, one imagines, in the SYNTHESIS OF INTENDED MEANING.
3. This is the sociological world in which we live! The National "conversation" on gender is almost entirely occupied by SYNTHETIC WISDOM. No matter the genetic composition of the individual, X and Y chromosomes mean nothing! A logical fact just maneuvered out of consideration! Anatomical structure is pronounced irrelevant! In the stead of facts, responses are SYNTHESIZED FROM EMOTION, IDEOLOGY, CONFUSION THROUGH SCHOOL CURRICULA and POSSIBLY SO CALLED "EXPERT" OPINION. This we may call SYNTHETIC WISDOM.
4. SYNTHETIC WISDOM IS a SATANIC TACTIC USED TO DECEIVE and CONFUSE. "... Indeed, has God said, 'You shall not eat from any tree of the garden?' Genesis 3:1. Eve corrected the "serpent", 3:2, 3.
5. God told Adam and Eve "... You shall not eat from it or touch it, (the forbidden tree) or you will die", 3:3. But the serpent interjected forcefully, "you surely will not die!" 3:4. Then he SYNTHESIZED "WISDOM", 3:5, from his knowledge of men, and of course his intent to cause distrust of REVELATION and the character of God.
6. In our political language, especially in its use TV comedians are almost exclusively SYNTHETIC!
7. The idea is to belittle, demean, diminish the integrity of SPIRITUAL REALITY. It is certainly contrived, calculated, or the term we suggest here: SYNTHESIZED.
8. Couple all this to the prevailing influence of what is called POSTMODERNISM, according to which there is no fixed truth, no objective reality and no master narratives, like the Bible.
9. We are awash in SYNTHETIC REASONING and its contrivances! Refer to Romans 1.

10. Consider this: "For since the creation of the world His (God) invisible attributes, His eternal power and divine nature, have been clearly seen, being understood through what has been made, so that they are without excuse", 1:20. Then comes a CONTRIVED SYNTHETIC RESPONSE: "For even though they knew God, they did not honor Him as God or give thanks, but they became futile in their speculations, and their foolish heart was darkened…Professing to be wise, they became fools", 1:21, 22.
11. We are always at war with SYNTHETIC WISDOM.

ADDITIONAL NOTES

Reflecting on Ezekiel:

What's the Main Point or Generalization this Lesson makes About Reality in this Book of the Bible?

CHANGEPOINTS

I think I need to change my view of reality to match God's in the following areas:

Make a list here of other verses in the book that deal with God's view of reality

1

2

3

4

5

6

7

8

From Ezekiel

THE STRUCTURE OF REALITY

1. Ezekiel was a man occupying space in time. He was located somewhere on the TEMPORAL TIMELINE. He was surrounded by specific HISTORICAL CONDITIONS.
2. "The word of the Lord came expressly to Ezekiel the priest, son of Buzi, in the land of the Chaldeans by the river Chebar; and there the hand of the Lord came upon him", 1:3.
3. That action instigated by INVISIBLE REALITY changes the whole fabric of life. The man on the spot learned that INVISIBLE REALITY was about to impose a different and radical structure upon time and materiality and upon the mind!
4. "As I looked behold, a storm wind was coming from the north, a great cloud with fire flashing forth continually and a bright light around it, and in its midst something like glowing metal in the midst of the fire."
5. We learn that TEMPORAL HISTORY becomes a vehicle for the GREAT UNSEEN. Then, Ezekiel was obliged to consider the RELATION BETWEEN THE VISIBLE ➡ and INVISIBLE: "Now above the expanse that was over their heads there was something resembling a throne, like lapis lazuli in appearance; and on that resembled a throne, high up, was a figure with the appearance of a man". "… Such was the appearance of the likeness of the glory of the Lord. And when I saw it, I fell on my face and heard a voice speaking", 1:26, 28.
6. All of that was a reaction to the "likeness" of the INVISIBLE REALITY: Not the actual GREAT ONE HIMSELF.
7. There is a LANGUAGE RELATION between the THREE DIMENSIONS OF REALITY. Two LEVELS OF INTELLIGENCE are in relation!
8. "Then He said to me, 'Son of man, stand on your feet that I may speak with you! As He spoke to me the Spirit entered me and set me on my feet; and I heard Him speaking to me", 2:1, 2. Ludwig Wittgenstein, an Austrian philosopher, came to the conclusion that human language cannot adequately communicate meaning from one mind to another. However, the Holy Spirit links the mind of God ➡ to the minds of men in time and that by the avenue of language!
9. There is a SUPERNATURAL LANGUAGE MANIFOLD given to men who believe and is relatable to the people of the world: "I am sending you to them who are stubborn and obstinate children, and you shall say to them, 'Thus says the Lord God'", 2:4. It is some men in time conveying

to other men in time, the REVEALED WORD OF GOD. And thus the INVISIBLE and the VISIBLE can be brought into contact!

10. SPIRITUAL TRANSFORMATION is in the ascendant: "Then He said to me, 'Son of man, eat what you find; eat this scroll, and go, speak to the house of Israel. So I opened my mouth, and He fed me this scroll. He said to me, 'Son of man, feed your stomach and fill your body with this scroll which I am giving you'. Then I ate it, and it was sweet as honey in my mouth", 3:1-3. The word is to be metabolized as personal sustenance! SPIRITUAL SUSTENANCE. This is also part of the STRUCTURE OF REALITY.

ADDITIONAL NOTES

Reflecting on Daniel:

What's the Main Point or Generalization this Lesson makes About Reality in this Book of the Bible?

CHANGEPOINTS

I think I need to change my view of reality to match God's in the following areas:

Make a list here of other verses in the book that deal with God's view of reality

1

2

3

4

5

6

7

8

From Daniel
THE STRUCTURE OF REALITY

1. Worldly thinkers like Friedrich Nietzsche and Ludwig Wittgenstein, now long gone, yet whose writings are considered important, made the argument that ANY SIGNIFICANT APPRAISAL OF HOW THE WORLD IS, MUST BE FOUNDED IN TIME and MATERIALITY.
2. Their idea was that human language is insufficient to "copy" the nature of "reality".
3. However, the Book of Daniel affirms the proposition that human language is not beyond the reach of God! AND THAT IS THE POINT.
4. "The Lord gave Jehoiakim king of Judah into his hand, along with some of the vessels of the house of God, and he brought them to the land of Shinar, to the house of his god, and he brought the vessels into the treasury of his god", 1:2. There are no supposed "laws of history" driving world events! It's the ALMIGHTY in the driver's seat!
5. The revealed language manifold put a line in the sand, Daniel stayed on the right side of that language! "But Daniel made up his mind that he would not defile himself… ", 1:8. Daniel had a choice to make, as do we all. Wherever his mind went, his body was going to follow!
6. The word of God was determinant over his behavior. The INVISIBLE PERSONAGE from heaven was shaping HUMAN COGNITIVE CONTENT: "As for these four youths (Daniel, Hananiah, Mishael, Azariah), God have them knowledge and intelligence in every branch of literature and wisdom; Daniel even understood all kinds of visions and dreams", 1:17.
7. The emperor, Nebuchadnezzar, his mind shaped by divine power, was being decisively influenced by INVISIBLE REALITY, 2:1-4.
8. The compassion of God translates into pragmatic, this-world effects… "so that they might request compassion from the God of heaven concerning this mystery (2:1-13), so that Daniel and his friends would not be destroyed with the rest of the wise men of Babylon", 2:18.
9. "But as for me, this mystery has not been revealed to me for any wisdom residing in me more than any other living man, but for the purpose of making the interpretation known to the king, and that you may understand the thoughts of your mind", 2:30.
10. Then inexplicable things began to happen, MIRACLES, 3:8-30, The mighty king of the Babylonians was compelled to rethink the STRUCTURE OF REALITY. "Nebuchadnezzar the king to all the peoples, nations and men of every language that live in all the earth: 'May your peace

abound!' It seemed good to me to declare the signs and wonders which the Most High God has done for me. How great are His signs and how mighty are His wonders! His kingdom is an everlasting kingdom and His dominion is from generation to generation, "4:1-3. Everything in biblical faith depends upon how one comprehends the STRUCTURE OF REALITY. That is why Daniel "... made up his mind that he would not defile himself... ", 1:8.

Meme from Representational Research artist Elizabeth Darnell. For information about terms, see the Glossary at RepresentationalResearch.com.

Reflecting on Hosea:

What's the Main Point or Generalization this Lesson makes About Reality in this Book of the Bible?

CHANGEPOINTS

I think I need to change my view of reality to match God's in the following areas:

Make a list here of other verses in the book that deal with God's view of reality

1

2

3

4

5

6

7

8

From Hosea

THE STRUCTURE OF REALITY

1. The Almighty required something very peculiar and unanticipated of Hosea: "When the Lord first spoke through Hosea, the Lord said to Hosea, 'Go, take to yourself a wife of harlotry and have children of harlotry; for the land commits flagrant harlotry, forsaking the Lord'", 1:2.
2. The commandment was to color every aspect of the prophet's life. For him life was not to be about bliss, happiness not personal fulfillment! His was a life of service.
3. Hosea married Gomer, a woman not committed to marriage nor to fidelity within marriage! They had four children together, 1:3, 4. In Gomer's heart she was never truly devoted to Hosea. She would go after other men and go so far as to abandon the home she had with Hosea.
4. The INVISIBLE GOD OF THE UNIVERSE, TIME and MATERIALITY HAD CALLED HOSEA TO LIVE THE EMBLEMATIC LIFE.
5. The EMBLEMATIC LIFE IS JUST THAT, a CALLING and it is per the will of God! The prophet's life was tragic, disappointing and painful, one imagines.
6. One might "feel" guilty for how things turned out, but nothing could have averted it! The marital relation between Hosea ➡ and Gomer was EMBLEMATIC of the relation between God ➡ and Israel! Above all it is a pictorial of HUMAN REDEMPTION.
7. Gomer turned away from her husband just as Israel had turned away from God! Why had this happened? The answer is found in how the offending parties grasped the STRUCTURE OF REALITY. Both Gomer, the EMBLEM of Israel as well as Israel herself had rejected the SPIRITUAL SUBSTRATE OF THE UNIVERSE and pursued only the things of the flesh! 2:5-8.
8. This means, among other things, that a believer caught up in an EMBLEMATIC LIFE that has engulfed them, must determine exactly how does one conceive of what is most REAL, the SPIRITUAL or the TEMPORAL? Obviously psychological counseling will not change one's understanding!
9. The EMBLEMATIC LIFE is inherently problematic and difficult. It will produce unhappiness! But it had a SUPERNATURAL PURPOSE.
10. Hosea goes out to buy Gomer back from her lovers, 3:1-5. Just as the Lord redeemed Israel, so Hosea emblematically redeemed his faithless wife. God was demonstrating His forgiveness and lovingkindness!

Hosea was not permitted to cut and run! He had to stay the course, endure the pain, redeem his wife and suffer as did the Almighty and forgive! Tough business this! Yet the Lord can call us to the EMBLEMATIC LIFE. To generate a picture of the relation between God ➡ and Time and the relation between men ➡ and the flesh!

ADDITIONAL NOTES

For an extensive study of what it means when God creates a symbol out of a person: https://www.representationalresearch.com/pdfs/EzekielComplete.pdf

Reflections on this Generalization:

NOTES

GENERALIZATION

THE STRUCTURE OF REALITY

1. Throughout the Scripture record, there is the clear understanding that the CENTRAL NERVOUS SYSTEM operates in direct opposition to faith in the word of God. Genesis 3 is the first instantiation of this practice. The "serpent" enticed Adam and Eve to trust in the performance of the five senses.
2. It occurred again in Egypt when the weight of faith was too onerous for the Israelites to bear. The faith performance of Israel was lackluster at the Red Sea, Exodus chapters 13, 14. And there are many other examples.
3. There are THREE STATES OF CONSCIOUSNESS THAT IMPINGE HERE: 1) RATIONALISM (dependence upon human rational capacity; 2) IRRATIONALITY (reacting to all things RATIONAL); 3) NON RATIONAL (something not developed by the minds of men.)
4. At Kadesh Barnea, Numbers 14, all three conditions were in play. When the reconnaissance mission by the 12 spies had been completed, the spies made their report to the assembled people of Israel.
5. Ten members of the reconnaissance party objected to what they thought to be a pretense of achieving any victory over the Canaanites. To pursue the invasion was to be IRRATIONAL. It made no sense; it was impossible they thought in Numbers 13.
6. The RATIONAL MIND could not comprehend the mission nor the foundation of the REVEALED PROMISE made to them centuries before!
7. God is not RATIONAL, as are men. His words to us are not Rational, they are, rather NON RATIONAL. They came not from the human mind but from the SUPERNATURAL MIND, transcending the limitation of human RATIONALITY.
8. In the contemporary, in many circumstances, human rationality overshadows and can overrule the REVEALED TRUTH.
9. It is not only possible but it can be likely that believers, by their rationalized reading of Scripture, can demonstrate more confidence in RATIONALISM than in the expressed will of God!
10. The Israelites during the Exodus and later proved the point: believers can fall into the trap of RATIONALIZED FAITH. That is in effect COUNTERFAITH.

Reflections on this Generalization:

NOTES

GENERALIZATION

THE STRUCTURE OF REALITY.

1. The practice of faith is an invitation to INVISIBLE REALITY to execute its will upon the TEMPORAL PART OF REALITY.
2. This principle is projected in the Old Testament Prophets and reiterated in the New Testament.
3. Jeremiah warned the people of God about the fact that the relation of the VISIBLE TO THE INVISIBLE is at the fulcrum of human history.
4. To neglect or otherwise reject this truth holds forbidding consequences. "Thus says the Lord, what injustice did your fathers find in Me, that they went far from Me and walked after emptiness and became empty? They did not say, 'Where is the Lord who brought us up out of the land of Egypt, who led us through the wilderness, through a land of deserts and of pits, through a land of drought and of deep darkness, through a land that no one crossed, and where no man dwelt?'" Jeremiah 2:5, 6.
5. No one can face the rigors of and the obstructions posed by the LOWER TEMPORAL ORDER OF REALITY on the foundation of SPIRITUAL EMPTINESS.
6. The New Testament book of James teaches the persistent truth that men must seek to draw the INVISIBLE REALITIES into relation with the VISIBLE.
7. The very definition of emptiness is to be devoid of any true and effective understanding of the index between the INVISIBLE ➡ and VISIBLE. Such a condition is the formula for debilitating depression and misunderstandings of REVEALED REALITY.
8. To be separated from the INVISIBLE REALITY heralds the end of civilization! "The vision of Isaiah the son of Amos concerning Judah and Jerusalem, which he saw during the reigns of Uzziah, Jotham, Ajax and Hezekiah kings of Judah. Listen O heavens and hear, O earth; for the Lord speaks, 'Sons I have reared and brought up, but they have revolted against Me'", Isaiah 1:1, 2
9. This state of being constitutes a COSMIC TRAGEDY. It appears that we are living through just such a COSMIC TRAGEDY in the present historical period!
10. Yet there is a way out! But it is singular. We must seek reunification with the INVISIBLE part of reality which brings with it the blessings of and the relief from "autonomous man"—which is a myth!

Reflecting on Joel:

What's the Main Point or Generalization this Lesson makes About Reality in this Book of the Bible?

CHANGEPOINTS

I think I need to change my view of reality to match God's in the following areas:

Make a list here of other verses in the book that deal with God's view of reality

1

2

3

4

5

6

7

8

From Joel

THE STRUCTURE OF REALITY

1. Joel asserts that INVISIBLE REALITY OVERSHADOWS the COMPLEX OF TEMPORAL VISIBLE REALITY.
2. The prophet speaks of a SUPERNATURAL INTERVENTION INTO THE TEMPORAL TIMELINE.
3. "Blow the trumpet in Zion, and sound an alarm on My holy mountain! Let all the inhabitants of the land tremble, for the day of the Lord is coming; surely it is near, a day of darkness and gloom, a day of clouds and thick darkness. As the dawn is spread over the mountains, so there is a great and mighty people; there has never been anything like it, nor will there be again after it to the years of many generations."
4. Not a new idea in scripture, but INVISIBLE REALITY is presented in Joel as PROTAGONIST! (a champion of a particular cause).
5. The Almighty is the CHAMPION OF SPIRITUALITY; and all things TEMPORAL are rooted in the spiritual!
6. In the contemporary, Spiritual Realities have, in general, lost all credibility! This has happened, even among churches. Governments demonstrate no acknowledgement of any responsibility toward unseen reality.
7. This spiritual deterioration leaves only one recourse for individuals as well as collectives: repentance and lamentation!
8. "… The day of the Lord is indeed great and very awesome, and who can endure it? Yet even now, declares the Lord, Return to Me with all your heart, and with fasting, weeping and mourning; and rend your heart and not your garments. Now return to the Lord your God, for He is gracious and compassionate, slow to anger, abounding in loving kindness and relenting of evil. Who knows whether He will not turn and relent and leave a blessing behind Him…", 2:11-14.
9. AS THE PROTAGONIST, the INVISIBLE LORD is the chief actor in human history! That truth displaces the primacy of situations, events, conditions and states of being!
10. The universe and our world within it is an OPEN SYSTEM. Those who deny the will of THE SUPERNATURAL PROTAGONIST must contend the everything that is seen, functions as a CLOSED SYSTEM! Nothing gets in from outside, they must conclude, and the VISIBLE IS ALL THAT THERE IS! Scripture, however, and everywhere contests that false premise! It is a FALSE STRUCTURE OF REALITY.

Reflecting on Amos:

What's the Main Point or Generalization this Lesson makes About Reality in this Book of the Bible?

CHANGEPOINTS

I think I need to change my view of reality to match God's in the following areas:

Make a list here of other verses in the book that deal with God's view of reality

1

2

3

4

5

6

7

8

From Amos

THE STRUCTURE OF REALITY

1. Heaven and earth are supremely distinct, as are the spiritual and the material.
2. However, the relation between the two spheres of reality is extremely strong and causal! We may employ the term "ORGANIC".
3. Like the arms and legs of the human body; those structures are ORGANIC to the body. The arms and legs grow out of the body. These parts of the body are of one piece with the body.
4. In the same way, Amos addresses the connection between spiritual ➡ and material, "... The Lord (spiritual) roars from Zion and from Jerusalem (material) He utters His voice; and the shepherds' pasture grounds mourn, and the summit of Carmel dries up", 1:2.
5. The two dimensions of reality are separate and they are not equal. "So I will send fire upon the house of Hazael and it will consume the citadels of Ben-Hadad", 1:4. What the spiritual decides materializes upon the temporal sphere! This is due to the ORGANIC RELATION between the two.
6. The causation, we may say, is non commutative. It moves in only one direction, from spiritual ➡ to temporal! The temporal sphere does not directly affect nor control the spiritual!
7. Because of this ORGANICISM, then, the fear of God is developed. This ORGANIC RELATION was the specific force behind the liberation of the Jews from Egyptian captivity. "It was I who brought you up from the land of Egypt, and I led you in the wilderness forty years that you may take possession of the Amorites", 2:10.
8. ORGANICISM is the driving force behind personal prayer! It appears that prayer occupies the nexus between God ➡ and Time! In other words, prayer has to do with the STRUCTURE OF REALITY.
9. ORGANIC RELATIONS HAVE A CERTAIN LOGIC: Two men ➡ and mutual appointments; a lion's roar ➡ and the presence of prey; birds fall into traps ➡ and if the trap is baited; a trumpet is blown ➡ people assemble; calamity happens ➡ and the Lord has done it, 3:3-6.
10. Believers should follow the divine logic: our reasoning, behavior and psychology should be ORGANIC RESPONSES to the character and nature of God and the spiritual dimension! This requires meditation.
11. Believers live in the recognition of this ORGANICISM. We depend upon it in all and every situation, event and state of being. It is the way the world is! Part of reality!

Reflections on this Generalization:

NOTES

GENERALIZATION

THE STRUCTURE OF REALITY

1. One of the lessons that we learn from the totality of the Scripture is this: THINGS ON THE MATERIAL/TEMPORAL SIDE ARE NOT AS DECISIVE AS THEY APPEAR TO BE.
2. The size, weaponry, and experience of Goliath of Gath turned out to be indecisive in his fight with King David, 1 Samuel 17.
3. It happened at Kadesh Barnea that the Israelites were intimidated by the number of soldiers and the fortified cities of Canaan and so they refused battle with the enemies of God, Numbers 13, 14.
4. The Israelites were habitually depressed and fearful of temporal material conditions. They were very convinced of the DECISIVENESS OF THOSE CONDITIONS.
5. We do find individuals who were more impressed with INVISIBLE REALITY THAN WITH VISIBLE REALITY. Take the Hebrew midwives of Moses' day, Exodus 1:15-22. Those women were more moved by the power of God than by the power of the state!
6. The psalmists were aware of material and naturalistic forces. Yet, they consistently appealed to INVISIBLE REALITIES.
7. "My voice rises to God, and I will cry aloud, my voice rises to God, and He will hear me. In the day of my trouble I sought the Lord… ", Psalm 77:1, 2.
8. Job was fully convinced that his faith had been well placed in the UNSEEN GOD. "Then the Lord said to Job, 'Will the faultfinder contend with the Almighty? Let him who reproved God answer it.' Then Job answered said, 'Behold, I am insignificant; what can I reply to You? I lay my hand on my mouth. Once I have spoken, and I will answer; Even twice, and I will add nothing more'", Job 40:1-3.
9. We, as believers, are to therefore be prepared to disregard what common sense and rational thought consider to be DECISIVE!
10. Any significant and or threatening health event is usually gauged on the foundation of DECISIVE MATERIAL ELEMENTS. But BIBLICAL FAITH changes all the rules! How we believers comprehend the STRUCTURE OF REALITY is prerequisite!

Reflecting on Obadiah:

What's the Main Point or Generalization this Lesson makes About Reality in this Book of the Bible?

CHANGEPOINTS

I think I need to change my view of reality to match God's in the following areas:

Make a list here of other verses in the book that deal with God's view of reality

1

2

3

4

5

6

7

8

From Obadiah

THE STRUCTURE OF REALITY

1. No man, no people is beyond the reach of INVISIBLE REALITY. SECULARISM is *de facto* denial of INVISIBLE REALITY.
2. In Obadiah, THE TARGET PEOPLE are the EDOMITES. "We have heard a report from the Lord, and an envoy has been sent among the nations saying, 'Arise and let us go against her for battle'" 1:1.
3. Invisible envoys were sent to observe and form an appraisal of Edom, how they live, how they think and how they see reality.
4. The Edomites believed that the right MATERIAL CIRCUMSTANCES amounted to security. This is a typical mistake or misconjecture!
5. They were mountain dwellers; hard to get to, in perfect defensive position. Their belief was that no known enemy posed a serious threat to them. "The arrogance of your heart has deceived you, you who live in the clefts of the rock, in the loftiness of your dwelling place, who say in your heart, who will bring me down to earth", 1:3.
6. The Edomites never suspected that they incurred an UNKNOWN and INVISIBLE ENEMY. There are several world nations that completely qualify as contemporary EDOMITES.
7. Some rest somewhat assured behind vast military establishments, thinking they are invulnerable! Yet an UNKNOWN, INVISIBLE and PURPOSED ENEMY IS JUDGING THEM and MOVING CLOSER TO THE ATTACK.
8. "Will I not on that day, declares the Lord, destroy wise men from Edom and understanding from the mountain of Esau? Then your mighty men will be dismayed, O Teman, so that everyone may be cut off from the mountain of Esau by slaughter", 1:8.
9. So INVISIBLE REALITY says, "Though you build high like the eagle, though you set your nest among the stars, from there I will bring you down, declares the Lord", 1:4.
10. Then, a final warning, "For the day of the Lord draws near on all the nations, as you have done, it will be done to you, your dealings will return on your own head", 1:15.

Reflecting on Jonah:

What's the Main Point or Generalization this Lesson makes About Reality in this Book of the Bible?

CHANGEPOINTS
I think I need to change my view of reality to match God's in the following areas:

Make a list here of other verses in the book that deal with God's view of reality

1

2

3

4

5

6

7

8

From Jonah

THE STRUCTURE OF REALITY

1. Jonah experienced a mental condition called COGNITIVE DISSONANCE (an extreme state of INCONSISTENCY).
2. Jonah knew the Lord was real and that He had spoken, yet Jonah immediately disobeyed.
3. "The word of the Lord came to Jonah… 'Arise, go to Nineveh that great city and cry against it, for their wickedness has come up before Me'. But Jonah rose up to flee to Tarshish from the presence of the Lord. So he went down to Joppa, found a ship which was going to Tarshish, paid the fare and went down into it to go with them to Tarshish from the presence of the Lord", 1:1-3.
4. One may doubt that Jonah was unaware of the omnipresence of God. But perhaps he thought that if he left the region in question that it would excuse him from the mission.
5. Knowing the revealed will of God, still Jonah chose to ignore it! That kind of blatant inconsistency was not tolerated by the SUPREME INVISIBLE REALITY.
6. No one escapes from the OMNIPRESENCE of the INVISIBLE ONE. Nor does anyone escape from REVEALED imperatives. We are all in the same boat regardless of the historical epoch in which we serve.
7. Jonah suffered COGNITIVE DISSONANCE as he knew the command of God and then chose not to surrender to it, in favor of clinging to his own PREFERENCES, WILL and PERSONAL WISDOM.
8. Not one of us is immune from the same inclination! When questioned about his behavior Jonah was candid: "But it greatly displeased Jonah and he became angry. He prayed to the Lord and said, 'Please Lord, was not this what I said while I was still in my own country? Therefore in order to forestall this I fled to Tarshish, for I knew that You are a gracious and compassionate God, slow to anger and abundant lovingkindness, and one who relents concerning calamity'", 4:1.
9. This was a clash between the CHARACTER OF GOD and the character of the prophet!
10. The INVISIBLE REALITY is PERSONAL— meaning that it is a PERSON. One who thinks and then translates what He thinks into action on the VISIBLE SIDE. There is nothing abstract about the INVISIBLE. We should not confuse INVISIBILITY for ABSTRACTION. For He is nothing of the sort!

11. He is the root of all and every good thing! He commands the seas and everything in them! He is the master of events! He is good, kind, just and true! And we are fully dependent upon His greatness!
12. WE ARE IN THE PRESENCE OF A MOST PROFOUND PERSONAGE, WELL BEYOND US. But we are not beyond His reach! That is REALITY.

Representation :

A way of symbolizing or conveying the idea of a fact.

Meme from Representational Research artist Elizabeth Darnell. For information about terms, see the Glossary at RepresentationalResearch.com.

Reflecting on Micah:

What's the Main Point or Generalization this Lesson makes About Reality in this Book of the Bible?

CHANGEPOINTS

I think I need to change my view of reality to match God's in the following areas:

Make a list here of other verses in the book that deal with God's view of reality

1

2

3

4

5

6

7

8

From Micah

THE STRUCTURE OF REALITY

1. From the INVISIBLE "Holy Temple", comes the MORAL/BEHAVIORAL RULES PRESCRIBED FOR THE ENTIRE HUMAN RACE. The ground of these behavioral norms is God Himself.
2. To make the case for this arrangement the prophet stipulates: "Hear all peoples, all of you; listen O earth and all it contains, and let the Lord God be a witness against you, the Lord from His Holy Temple. For behold the Lord is coming forth from His place. He will come down and tread on the high places of the earth", 1:2, 3.
3. THE HUMAN RACE IS ON TRIAL. This judiciary analogy must, therefore, precede and displace "CULTURAL NORMS".
4. No such humanly developed practices possess any autonomy in the living presence of the occupant of the Holy Temple!
5. The Structure of Reality had been willingly warped, being fomented by the phenomenon of Idolatry. "All her idols will be smashed, all of her earnings will be burned with fire, all of her images I will make desolate, for she collected them from a harlot's earnings, and to the earnings of a harlot they will return", 1:7.
6. Idolatry is an attempt to generate a FALSE STRUCTURE OF REALITY, involving origins, nature and a definition of the normal!
7. Mankind, however, is not free to arbitrarily construct the edifice of Reality! And that is precisely what is happening all over the world. The Chinese are attempting to construct a new reality based on their government's terroristic relation to the entire world; Antifa and BLM are trying to construct new social realities founded on their own arbitrary preconceptions and violence. In other words, terrorism! Gender activists have their very own arbitrary visions of reality—and that founded upon their demand to be allowed to plot visions of Reality founded upon their requirement that there *is no* objective Reality.
8. Military thinkers have said that "no military strategy can survive contact with the enemy". Because the enemy will react and adjust to the plan forcing adjustments to the original battle plan!
9. Another may consider that no false ideology of reality can survive contact with the Biblical Revealed picture of Reality. That is Micah's understanding! "The mountains will melt under Him and the valleys will be split, like wax before the fire, like water poured down a steep place", 1:4.

10. From within the Kingdom of God believers breathe out a defiant message: "But as for me, I will watch expectantly for the Lord; I will wait for the God of my salvation, my God will hear me. Do not rejoice over me, O my enemy. Though I fall I will rise; though I dwell in darkness, the Lord is a light for me", 7:7, 8.

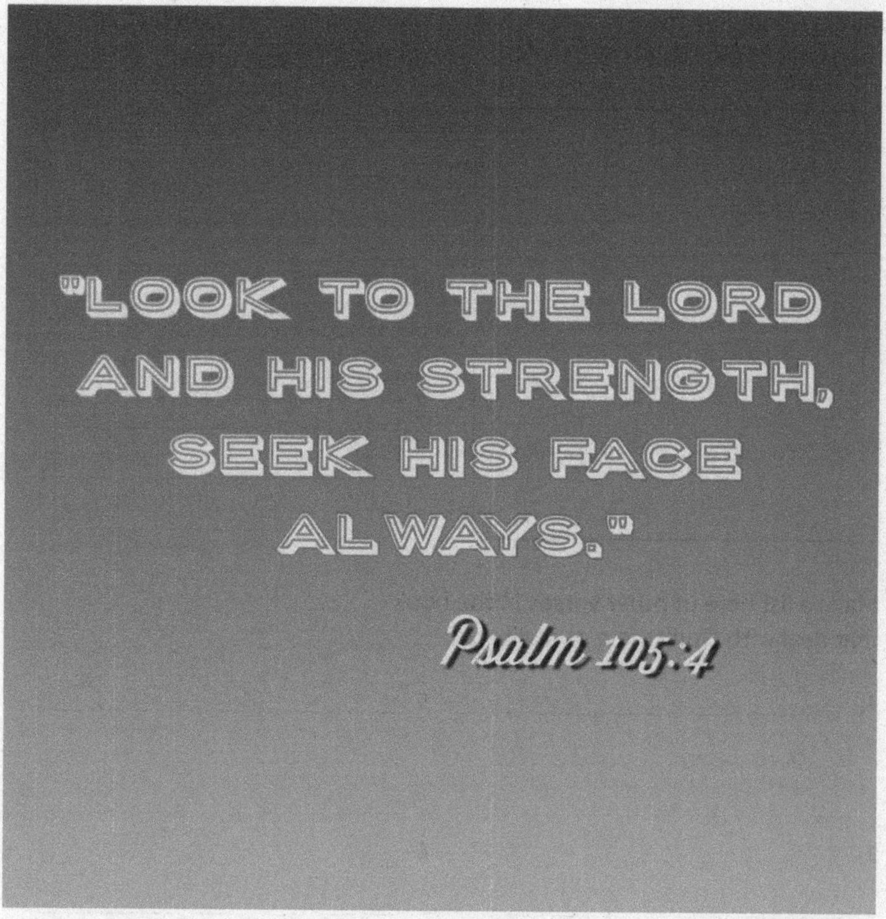

Meme from Representational Research artist Elizabeth Darnell. For information about terms, see the Glossary at RepresentationalResearch.com.

Reflecting on Nahum:

What's the Main Point or Generalization this Lesson makes About Reality in this Book of the Bible?

CHANGEPOINTS

I think I need to change my view of reality to match God's in the following areas:

Make a list here of other verses in the book that deal with God's view of reality

1

2

3

4

5

6

7

8

From Nahum

THE STRUCTURE OF REALITY

1. The INVISIBLE REALITY being PERSONAL, then, possesses certain PERSONALITY TRAITS and with those men must contend!
2. "A jealous and avenging God is the Lord; the Lord is avenging and wrathful. The Lord takes vengeance on His adversaries, and He reserves wrath for His enemies", 1:2.
3. INVISIBLE REALITY acts as COUNTER AGENCY to human machinations: "Whatever you devise against the Lord, He will make a complete end of it. Distress will not rise up twice", 1:9.
4. Any enemy of God will put himself between the Almighty ➡ and those who try to live by Revealed Truth!
5. Nineveh was just such an organized and sociological enemy. They organized themselves to resist the SPIRITUAL REALITIES. "Woe to the bloody city, completely full of lies and pillage; His prey never departs", 3:1.
6. There are many cities and many countries who have adopted the tactics of ancient Nineveh. They are unalterably opposed to any REVEALED SPIRITUALITY.
7. These are oppressive collectives who stand between God and those who follow Him! However, the prophet warns that they will face a superior intelligence and force determined to fence them in and then, destroy them!
8. These words should be considered an existential threat to all the enemies of the INVISIBLE REALITY: "Behold, I am against you, declares the Lord of hosts. 'I will burn up her chariots in smoke, a sword will devour your young lions; I will cut off your prey from the land, and no longer will the voice of your messengers be heard'", 2:13.
9. The enemies of God have no true advantage! Their doom has already been arranged! Their visions will fail them, their presumptions were overmatched by SUPERNATURAL ANGER.

Reflecting on Habakkuk:

What's the Main Point or Generalization this Lesson makes About Reality in this Book of the Bible?

CHANGEPOINTS

I think I need to change my view of reality to match God's in the following areas:

Make a list here of other verses in the book that deal with God's view of reality

1

2

3

4

5

6

7

8

From Habakkuk

THE STRUCTURE OF REALITY.

1. The INVISIBLE REALITY is the generatrix of TEMPORAL HISTORY. All philosophies of history except one (the BIBLICAL ONE) are wrong.
2. Hegel, Spangler, Marx and others were hopelessly under-dimensioned!
3. "The oracle which Habakkuk saw. How long, O Lord, will I call for help, and you will not hear? I cry out to You, Violence! Yet You do not save", 1:1, 2.
4. TEMPORAL HISTORY was not developing as the prophet thought best! He appealed to God (INVISIBLE REALITY) but nothing was corrected nor reversed!
5. It was revealed to the prophet that God Himself was driving the shaping of TEMPORAL HISTORY.
6. "Look among the nations! Observe! Be astonished! Wonder! Because I am doing something in your days—You would not believe if you were told", 1:5.
7. The times were hard, stressful, disappointing, and dangerous, 1:6-11. And all of that was playing out under the auspices of a superior reality: "Are You not from everlasting, O Lord, my God, my Holy One? We will not die. You, O Lord, have appointed them to judge; and You, O Rock, have established them to correct", 1:12.
8. There are two kinds of people who live through those tremulous times. 1) one is proud, whose "… soul is not right within him" and 2) "… the righteous (who) will live through it by (their) faith", 2:4.
9. The Lord had a purpose in His arrangement of TEMPORAL HISTORY. "For the vision is yet for the appointed time; It hastens toward the goal and it will not fail. Though it tarries, wait for it; for it will certainly come, it will not delay", 2:3.
10. We do not always know what is going on! And it might be unnerving! But we consider the organizer of TEMPORAL HISTORY. Habakkuk prayed, "Lord, I have heard the report about You and I fear. O Lord, revive Your work in the midst of the years, In the midst of the years make it known", 3:2.

Reflecting on Zephaniah:

What's the Main Point or Generalization this Lesson makes About Reality in this Book of the Bible?

CHANGEPOINTS

I think I need to change my view of reality to match God's in the following areas:

Make a list here of other verses in the book that deal with God's view of reality

1

2

3

4

5

6

7

8

From Zephaniah

THE STRUCTURE OF REALITY

1. The authority of the INVISIBLE REALITY is without peer.
2. "I will completely remove all things from the face of the earth, declares the Lord", 1:2.
3. His power and autonomy of action cannot be compared with anything natural! We are dealing with a MAGNITUDE OF REALITY beyond any TEMPORAL DIMENSION. We are in over our heads and beyond human possibilities of containment!
4. An event is predicted, foretold really, and mankind is to live in its shadow! "Be silent before the Lord God! For the day of the Lord is near, for the Lord has prepared a sacrifice, He has consecrated His guests", 1:7.
5. There will be no avoidance, no place to hide, nowhere to run! "It will come about at that time that I will search Jerusalem with lamps, and I will punish the men who are stagnant in spirit, who say in their hearts, the Lord will not do good or evil ", 1:12.
6. There are philosophies, ideologies actually, which attempt to depose the Almighty of His power and His word. They think of Him as inert! Not doing good nor evil! Zephaniah warns that they are wrong, untutored in the GREATER REALITY. Because TEMPORAL REALITY IS ALL THAT THERE IS, or so they believe!
7. All that such people have striven for and delighted in and that insulated would simply collapse! All their pursuits will be exhibited as empty, meaningless! "Neither their silver nor their gold will be able to deliver them on the day of the Lord's wrath; and all the earth will be devoured in the fire of His jealousy, for He will make a complete end, indeed a terrifying one, of all the inhabitants of the earth", 1:18.
8. There is a remedy for the coming debacle: "Seek the Lord, all you humble of the earth who have carried out His ordinances; seek righteousness, seek humility. Perhaps you will be hidden in the day of the Lord's anger", 2:3. Men are not of the same MAGNITUDE AS THAT OF GOD. We must not make any such pretense in thought, speech or behavior!
9. The citizen of the INVISIBLE REALITY is admonished and given guidance. "I said 'Surely you will revere Me, accept instruction.' So her dwelling will not be cut off according to all that I have appointed concerning her. But they were eager to corrupt all their deeds. THEREFORE WAIT FOR ME, declares the Lord, for the day when I rise up as a witness", 3:7-8.

10. A day of coming exaltation is in the pipeline! So, "Shout for joy, O daughter of Zion! Shout in triumph, O Israel! Rejoice and exult with all your heart, O daughter of Jerusalem", 3:14.
11. Today isn't all there is! The "here and now" isn't all there is, our trials, pains and ordeals are not all there is, our sufferings are in the course of the ETERNAL WILL coming to an end! Says the mighty One of the INVISIBLE REALITY.

FACT:

A fact is something that can be represented.

Examples:
person, object, circumstance, event

Meme from Representational Research artist Elizabeth Darnell. For information about terms, see the Glossary at RepresentationalResearch.com.

Reflecting on Haggai:

What's the Main Point or Generalization this Lesson makes About Reality in this Book of the Bible?

CHANGEPOINTS

I think I need to change my view of reality to match God's in the following areas:

Make a list here of other verses in the book that deal with God's view of reality

1

2

3

4

5

6

7

8

From Haggai

THE STRUCTURE OF REALITY

1. The INVISIBLE REALITY demands the personal transformation of the people of the earth and that especially applies to those who claim to be the people of God.
2. "Thus says the Lord of hosts, 'Consider your ways!'", 1:7.
3. The record shows that the people in question were self-involved, self-absorbed, carnal and negligent of spiritual realities!
4. "Thus says the Lord of hosts, this people says, 'The time has not come even the time for the house of the Lord to be built'", 1:2. Time had been wasted and invested in their self-indulgence: The prophet brought the word of divine disapproval! "Is it time for you yourselves to dwell in your paneled houses while this house lies desolate?" 1:4.
5. This necessarily means that the ETERNAL REALITY holds controlling interest in the human personal use of time! Time and materiality are the junior members!
6. Men will use time in personal pursuits or out of reverence for God, and act accordingly: "Then Zerubbabel the son of Shealtiel and Joshua the son of Jehozadak, the high priest, with all the remnant of the people, obeyed the voice of the Lord their God and the words of Haggai the prophet, as the Lord their God had sent him. And the people showed reverence for the Lord", 1:12.
7. The people turned back to God as their consciences CONTRACTED back upon the INVISIBLE REALITY. Transformation was the new agenda! They could not go on as they had before!
8. Then came the good news: "Then Haggai the messenger of the Lord, spoke by the commission of the Lord to the people saying, 'I am with you,' declares the Lord'", 1:13. The determinant approval of the INVISIBLE REALITY was restored and with it came all of its blessings!
9. The people were SUPERNATURALLY INVIGORATED: "So the Lord stirred up the spirit of Zerubbabel... and the spirit of Joshua... and the spirit of all the remnant of the people; and they came and worked on the house of the Lord of hosts, their God", 1:14. Just there is the secret of unity and revival! It is close proximity between the people ➡ and their God.
10. That work was somewhat dangerous but the Almighty addressed that very circumstance: "'But now take courage, Zerubbabel, declares the Lord, take courage also, Joshua... and all you people of the land take

courage', declares the Lord, 'and work; for I am with you', declares the Lord... My Spirit is abiding in your midst, do not fear!'", 2:4, 5.

11. The INVISIBLE REALITY does not leave itself inert nor mute in TEMPORAL MATTERS. The Lord is quite taken with the thought, speech and behavior of people on the VISIBLE SIDE OF REALITY.

FACT:

A fact is something that can be represented.

Meme from Representational Research artist Elizabeth Darnell. For information about terms, see the Glossary at RepresentationalResearch.com.

Reflecting on Zechariah:

What's the Main Point or Generalization this Lesson makes About Reality in this Book of the Bible?

CHANGEPOINTS

I think I need to change my view of reality to match God's in the following areas:

Make a list here of other verses in the book that deal with God's view of reality

1

2

3

4

5

6

7

8

From Zechariah

THE STRUCTURE OF REALITY

1. INVISIBLE REALITY CAN REACT. "The Lord was very angry with your fathers", 1:2.
2. Under such HISTORICAL CONDITIONS as the ANGER OF GOD, SOMETHING MUST BE DONE. "Therefore say to them, 'Thus says the Lord of hosts, Return to Me, declares the Lord of hosts, 'that I May return to you,' says the Lord of hosts", 1:3.
3. There was EXISTENTIAL DANGER in their chosen behavior! At any moment, "... the words, My statutes... ", could very well "overtake" any rebellious people and or individual!
4. Zechariah reports that INVISIBLE REALITY had at its disposal a spiritual and still invisible HORSE PLATOON "... to patrol the earth", 1:7-11.
5. We are not alone here! The most dangerous enemy any people can have is the God of the Bible, especially when He is angry! He can strike without further warning!
6. But the INVISIBLE GOD CAN BE FULLY GRACIOUS. "Therefore thus says the Lord, 'I will return to Jerusalem with compassion; my house will be built in it, declares the Lord of hosts, and a measuring line will be stretched over Jerusalem'", 1:16.
7. Then a most remarkable set of words followed: "And behold, the angel who was speaking with me was going out, and another angel was coming out to meet him, ... Run, speak to that young man, saying, 'Jerusalem will be inhabited without walls because of the multitude of men and cattle within it. For I, declares the Lord, will be a wall of fire around her, and I will be the glory in her midst'", 2:3-5.
8. The Inhabitant of Invisible Reality rules in the TEMPORAL ORDER OF REALITY: "... Not by might nor by power, but by My Spirit says the Lord of hosts", 4:6.
9. THE TEMPORAL REALITY EXISTS IN A VERY UNIQUE CONTEXT, and that is one of the messages of Zechariah! "... These are the four spirits of heaven, going forth after standing before the Lord of all the earth", 6:5.
10. Then, came a strong admonition: "Thus says the Lord of hosts, 'Let your hands be strong, you who are listening in those days to those words from the mouth of the prophets, those who spoke in the day that the foundation of the house of the Lord of hosts was laid, to the end that the temple might be built'", 8:9.
11. The Almighty is focused upon TEMPORAL REALITY. He is Judge, protector and the wall of surrounding His people!

Reflecting on Malachi:

What's the Main Point or Generalization this Lesson makes About Reality in this Book of the Bible?

CHANGEPOINTS

I think I need to change my view of reality to match God's in the following areas:

Make a list here of other verses in the book that deal with God's view of reality

1

2

3

4

5

6

7

8

From Malachi

THE STRUCTURE OF REALITY

1. The INVISIBLE REALITY spoke through Malachi, a mere man. The Lord reiterated, "I have loved you, says the Lord. But you say, 'How have You loved us?'" 1:2.
2. The people of Israel had grown to doubt the reliability of God! Still God was yet active in the affairs of men in time and materiality. The prophet made them a promise: "Your eyes will see this and you will say, 'The Lord be magnified beyond the border of Israel'", 1:5.
3. INVISIBLE REALITY had become superfluous and God had become "despise(d)… . O priests who despise My name. But you say, 'How have we despised Your name?'", 1:6.
4. In other words, men in time and materiality were expected to acknowledge their subordination to HIGHER REALITY independent of one's psychology!
5. All SYMBOLIC MEANING had evaporated! "The table of the Lord is to be despised", 1:7. The people felt free to offer sacrifices that were unacceptable to THE INVISIBLE REALITY.
6. Israel was in trouble with the true governance of the universe— CONTRADICTION HAD TO BE INTRODUCED INTO THE SITUATION: "'But now will you not entreat God's favor (faith must return), that He may be gracious to us? With such an offering on your part will He receive any of you kindly?' says the Lord of hosts", 1:9.
7. INVISIBLE REALITY had fallen out of favor with the people of God! "You also say, 'My, how tiresome it is! And you disdainfully sniff at it, says the Lord of hosts, and you bring what was taken by robbery and what is lame or sick; so you bring the offering! Should I receive that from your hand? says the Lord'", 1:13.
8. The Lord intended and still intends to confront men, women, boys and girls in time and materiality! And He means business; "If you do not listen, and if you do not take to heart to give honor to My name, says the Lord of hosts, then I will send the curse upon you and I will curse your blessings; and indeed, I have cursed them already, because you are not taking to heart", 2:2.
9. Israel was intended to be an INDEX (bridge) to the world! They had miserably failed! "True instruction was in his mouth and unrighteousness was not found on his lips; he walked with Me in peace and uprightness, and he turned many back from iniquity", 2:6.
10. Those are some of the PRECONDITIONS for our acceptance!

Reflecting on Matthew:

What's the Main Point or Generalization this Lesson makes About Reality in this Book of the Bible?

CHANGEPOINTS

I think I need to change my view of reality to match God's in the following areas:

Make a list here of other verses in the book that deal with God's view of reality

1

2

3

4

5

6

7

8

New Testament

From Matthew

THE STRUCTURE OF REALITY

1. In chapter one there is a list of generations, 1:1-17, demonstrative of the idea that time, history and life are always in a STATE OF CONTRACTION BACK UPON THE WILL OF GOD.
2. INVISIBLE REALITY is constantly pressing its purposes into the social structure of the world! Individual men are conscripted by the Lord to accomplish His will. The Son of God was to be inserted into the human timeline at a specific point in history. There was, of course, nothing natural about that!
3. A man named Joseph was drafted to serve as His earthly father. There were complications, 1:18-25. But Joseph was guided by UNSEEN REALITY through the difficulty: "Now the birth of Jesus Christ was as follows: when His mother Mary had been betrothed to Joseph, before they came together she was found to be with child by the Holy Spirit", 1:18.
4. Scandal was brewing. Joseph was being used by God but he was greatly troubled! He "… planned to send her away secretly", 1:19.
5. However, "… when he considered this, behold, an angel of the Lord appeared to him in a dream saying, 'Joseph, son of David, do not be afraid to take Mary as your wife; for the Child who has been conceived in her is of the Holy Spirit", 1:20.
6. Such things are "impossible" in the TEMPORAL ORDER OF REALITY. Or not! INVISIBLE REALITY can "manage" the circumstances of man. Such circumstances have no autonomy before the Almighty!
7. History was being directed by INVISIBLE REALITY. No intuition could fathom what was happening!
8. Herod's murder of the innocents was an affront to the UNSEEN REALITY — YET WAS NOT STOPPED BY IT, 2:16-23. The Son of God faced the temptations of this world but on SUPERNATURAL TERMS, 4:1-11. *One set of meanings was displaced by another*. Enhanced meanings were delivered deliberately into human sociology, 5:1-12.
9. The relation of God to materiality was one of power, and the relation of men to God was suppliance. The relations between the INVISIBLE ➡ and the VISIBLE are not symmetrical nor are they commutative! CAUSATION moves in only one singular direction!

10. What men would call an alien presence was and is, in fact, the true reality and source of redemption: “Behold, I send you out as sheep in the midst of wolves; so be shrewd as serpents and innocent as doves. But beware of men, for they will hand you over to the courts and scourge you in their synagogues; and you will even be brought before governors and kings for My sake, as a testimony to them and to the Gentiles. But when they hand you over, do not worry about how or what you are to say; for it will be given you in that hour what you are to say”, 10:16-19.

Representation :

A way of symbolizing or conveying the idea of a fact.

3 Types:

Iconic, Indexic, Linguistic

Meme from Representational Research artist Elizabeth Darnell. For information about terms, see the Glossary at RepresentationalResearch.com.

Reflecting on Mark:

What's the Main Point or Generalization this Lesson makes About Reality in this Book of the Bible?

CHANGEPOINTS

I think I need to change my view of reality to match God's in the following areas:

Make a list here of other verses in the book that deal with God's view of reality

1

2

3

4

5

6

7

8

From Mark

THE STRUCTURE OF REALITY.

1. The VISIBLE PART OF REALITY IS NOT IMPERMEABLE TO THE INVISIBLE REALITY.
2. To God, the two are one! "The beginning of the gospel of Jesus Christ, the Son of God.", 1:1.
3. Mark has often been described as a book of action and consequently aimed at the Roman/Gentile thinkers who preferred anything actionable. But it is just as easy to say that the miracles recorded in this book were preserved in memory for the precise purpose of demonstrating the SUPERNATURAL RELATION EXISTING BETWEEN THE INVISIBLE ➡ and THE VISIBLE.
4. How is it possible to reconnoiter the relation of God ➡ to time and materiality without the study of the miracles? And that relation is one of POWER.
5. On this foundation, then it becomes necessary to pursue the APPROVAL OF THE INVISIBLE REALITY. "In those days Jesus came from Nazareth in Galilee and was baptized by John in the Jordan. Immediately coming up out of the water, He saw the heavens opening, and the Spirit like a dove descending upon Him; and a voice came out of the heavens: 'You are My beloved Son, in You I am well-pleased'", 1:9-11.
6. Mark also contends that the entire panoply of nature is subject to INVISIBLE REALITY, 2:1-13. That fact offers significant implications for the practice of human reason and its dependence on "rationality."
7. The MIRACLE OF THE LOAVES and FISHES IS A PERFECT ILLUSTRATION OF THE FAITH PROBLEM WE CONFRONT IN THE CONTEMPORARY. When great crowds followed Jesus to listen to His wisdom, the crowd became hungry. And it was late in the day. The disciples suggested that the crowd disperse to get food for themselves! Jesus said, "You (the disciples) give them something to eat!", 6:37. That was beyond the power of the disciples to do! Then Jesus was presented 5 loaves and two fish (6:38) and then He…
8. "… took the five loaves and the two fish, and looking up toward heaven, He blessed the food and broke the loaves and He kept giving them to the disciples to set before them; and He divided up he two fish among them all", 6:41. Everyone ate to their satisfaction and afterward 5000 men ate the food. There is no indication that Jesus replicated the loaves and fish! He miraculously extended the mass of the bread and the fishes!

9. Jesus left the shore walking on the water, 6:45-48. The disciples saw Him and thought Him to be a "ghost", 6:49, 50. The disciples' understanding of the STRUCTURE OF REALITY had not changed! Not one bit! The disciples had witnessed the full miracle and knew that there was no natural, "rational" explanation! Yet their perception of REALITY never changed. Why? Because "… they had not gained any insight from the incident of the loaves, but their heart was hardened", 6:52.
10. This tells us that with the appearance of Jesus in the TEMPORAL ORDER, one's comprehension of the meaning of REALITY must accord with the chief representative of the UNSEEN PART OF REALITY. True faith cannot develop without that change!

Representation :

Representations are the only access we have to the physical world.

Meme from Representational Research artist Elizabeth Darnell. For information about terms, see the Glossary at RepresentationalResearch.com.

Reflecting on Luke:

What's the Main Point or Generalization this Lesson makes About Reality in this Book of the Bible?

CHANGEPOINTS

I think I need to change my view of reality to match God's in the following areas:

Make a list here of other verses in the book that deal with God's view of reality

1

2

3

4

5

6

7

8

From Luke

THE STRUCTURE OF REALITY

1. In the relation between INVISIBLE ➡ and VISIBLE REALITY, the burden of proof rests upon the INVISIBLE. "The angel answered and said to him (Zacharias), 'I am Gabriel, who stands in the presence of God, and I have been sent to speak to you and to bring you this good news. And behold, you shall be silent and unable to speak until the day when these things take place, because you did not believe my words, which will be fulfilled in their proper time",1:19, 20.
2. The INVISIBLE REALITY is by nature INTERVENTIONIST. "Gabriel was sent from God to a city in Galilee called Nazareth, to a virgin engaged to a man whose name was Joseph… and the virgin's name was Mary… he said to her, 'Greetings, favored one! The Lord is with you'. But she was very perplexed at this statement, and kept pondering what kind of salutation this was… .'Behold, you will conceive in your womb and bear a son, and you shall name Him Jesus'", 1:26-31.
3. A highly unlikely event was stipulated! The NATURAL ORDER OF CONCEPTION was to be bypassed! So, she was told, the Holy Spirit determines the course of VISIBLE REALITY, 1:35.
4. Gabriel contradicted all known knowledge of the universe: "For nothing will be impossible with God", 1:37. We must reconfigure our grasp of the relation between INVISIBLE ➡ and VISIBLE REALITY. Time and materiality are not determinant!
5. CAUSATION is a function of INVISIBLE REALITY, 1:46-56. All CAUSATION FLOWS FROM THE UNSEEN!
6. Jesus was born and He… "continued to grow and become strong, increasing in wisdom; and the grace of God was upon Him", 2:40. An alien to earth and among His own people, He was isolated in many ways because of His origin and relation to HIGHER ORDER REALITY.
7. In the temple and in dialogue with the learned He distinguished Himself: "And all who heard Him were amazed at His understanding and His answers", 2:47. His wisdom was not sociological, cultural nor temporal. Jesus raised the bar for wisdom!
8. Jesus knew His ORIENTATION IN THE TEMPORAL lower ORDER OF REALITY: "The Spirit of the Lord is upon Me, because He anointed Me to preach the gospel to the poor. He had sent Me to proclaim release to the captives, and recovery of sight to the blind, to set free those who are oppressed, to proclaim the favorable year of the Lord ", 4:18.

9. His ways on earth constituted a dissent from accepted wisdom! A new authority had come to Israel: John the Baptist had to be corrected and assured: ... "'Go and report to John what you have seen and heard: the blind receive sight, the lame walk, the lepers are cleansed, and the deaf hear, the dead are raised up, the poor have the gospel preached to them'", 7:22.
10. Miracles were done and in the end: death was defeated, 24:1-12. Jesus showed His relation to time and materiality and it was POWER!

Fact :

A fact can be represented in many ways.

Meme from Representational Research artist Elizabeth Darnell. For information about terms, see the Glossary at RepresentationalResearch.com.

Reflecting on John:

What's the Main Point or Generalization this Lesson makes About Reality in this Book of the Bible?

CHANGEPOINTS

I think I need to change my view of reality to match God's in the following areas:

Make a list here of other verses in the book that deal with God's view of reality

1

2

3

4

5

6

7

8

From John

THE STRUCTURE OF REALITY

1. John takes the mind back, even before the "beginning". The Gospel of John begins with a version of REALITY.
2. "In the beginning was the word, and the word was with God, and the word was God", 1:1. Nothing comes from nothing. Before there was anything there was God! So John presents God as the sole source of CAUSATION. And there was an eminence present called the "Logos" (translated as "the word") already there. The "Logos" constitutes a regime of authority!
3. INVISIBLE REALITY was in attendance and in complete charge of the CREATION SEQUENCE. And that "Logos" was a person. A SUPER INTELLIGENCE.
4. All designs originated in the mind of the "Logos". "He was in the beginning with God", 1:2. And Jesus was and is that "Logos". Then, John says something quite majestic about Jesus the "Logos": "All things came into being through Him, and apart from Him nothing came into being that has come into being", 1:3.
5. Without Jesus there would have been no CREATION as it is! The PRE-CONDITIONS FOR THE EXISTENCE OF THE UNIVERSE WERE INVISIBLE and SPIRITUAL. They were not physical, material nor KINETIC.
6. "In Him was life, and the life was the light of men", 1:4. Men are, therefore, much more than flesh and blood! There is a kind of light within them. And that, antagonistic to darkness!
7. In other words, men were created as vessels to bear into their world a kind of light that originated in God, in the invisible and particularly in Jesus the Supreme and immediate MASTER OF THE UNIVERSE.
8. It can only be that men represent the pinnacle of divine creation. People are created in the light of INVISIBLE REALITY. That sets us apart from the rest of creation! But Jesus was the light of lights. He came miraculously into the time continuum and in the form of flesh! He was a man and quite a bit more! "The light shines in the darkness, and the darkness did not grasp it", 1:5.
9. The "beginning" had no natural causation and no natural explanation! The VISIBLE REALITY IS THE PRODUCT OF THE TOTALLY INVISIBLE.
10. But Jesus was SPECIAL CASE. He came into the world to represent the ETERNAL and INVISIBLE REALITY. That was His mission! He presented a temporal and noticeable SYMBOL OF THE ROOT REALITY behind everything else that now surrounds us!

Reflecting on Acts:

What's the Main Point or Generalization this Lesson makes About Reality in this Book of the Bible?

CHANGEPOINTS

I think I need to change my view of reality to match God's in the following areas:

Make a list here of other verses in the book that deal with God's view of reality

1

2

3

4

5

6

7

8

From Acts

THE STRUCTURE OF REALITY

1. "And after He had said these things, He was lifted up while they were looking on, and a cloud received Him out of their sight. And as they were gazing intently into the sky while He was going, behold, two men in white clothing stood beside them. They also said, 'Men of Galilee, why do you stand looking into the sky? This Jesus, who has been taken up from you into heaven, will come in just the same way as you watched Himo g into heaven", 1:9-11.
2. How overpowering this event must have been to behold! In that place and at that time the margins between INVISIBLE ➡ and VISIBLE had all but disappeared!
3. The accounts with Judas Iscariot were settled. That man had betrayed the only true representative of the INVISIBLE REALITY. Prophecy recorded: "'Let His homestead be made desolate, and let no one dwell in it; let another man take his place'", 1:20.
4. "Pentecost" was upon them suddenly. And on that day, the margins between INVISIBLE ➡ and VISIBLE WERE EVEN MORE RECESSIVE—the INVISIBLE manifested itself noticeable, to say the least: "And suddenly there came from heaven a noise like a violent rushing wind, and it filled the whole house where they were sitting, and there appeared to them tongues as of fire distributing themselves, and they rested on each one of them. And they were all filled with the Holy Spirit and began to speak with other tongues, as the Spirit was giving them utterance", 2:1-4.
5. Something and/or Someone else had taken charge of events! No human being was directing the circumstances! It was purely SUPERNATURAL.
6. The will of heaven was accomplishing its purpose, 2:17-21. IT WOULD NOT BE DENIED. Men of great spiritual gravity knew that the spiritual realities are the only reliable foundation for personal existence: "... David says of Him, I saw the Lord always in my presence; for He is at my right hand so that I will not be shaken", 2:25.
7. Peter and John healed a crippled man and that by the power of God, 3:1-10. The fact did not pass inadvertently! INVISIBLE REALITY had come too close for that.
8. The gospel was preached and it was hard hitting, scathing and filled with rebuke! Disciples were subsequently arrested, interrogated and beaten, 3:11-4:31.

9. However, INVISIBLE REALITY took things well in hand! One of the scholars of the Jewish law, one "Gamaliel" spoke particularly about the relation between INVISIBLE ➡ and VISIBLE REALITY. He spoke in a very dangerous and tense moment!
10. "'… take care what you propose to do with these men… So in the present case, I say to you, stay away from these men and let them alone, for if this plan or action is of men, it will be overthrown; but if it is of God, you will not be able to overthrow them; or else you may even be found fighting against God'", 5:35-39.
11. INVISIBLE REALITY IS ALONE DETERMINANT IN HUMAN AFFAIRS and EVENTS.

Representational Research

To help people look at the way they represent the facts of their lives.

Meme from Representational Research artist Elizabeth Darnell. For information about terms, see the Glossary at RepresentationalResearch.com.

Reflecting on Romans:

What's the Main Point or Generalization this Lesson makes About Reality in this Book of the Bible?

CHANGEPOINTS

I think I need to change my view of reality to match God's in the following areas:

Make a list here of other verses in the book that deal with God's view of reality

1

2

3

4

5

6

7

8

From Romans

THE STRUCTURE OF REALITY

1. The apostle makes a succinct statement regarding the STRUCTURE OF REALITY: "For the wrath of God is revealed from heaven against all ungodliness and unrighteousness of men who suppress the truth in unrighteousness, because that which is known about God is evident within them; for God made it evident to them", 1:18, 19.
2.
   - There is a living and moral relation between the INVISIBLE ➡ and VISIBLE. SUPERNATURAL WRATH, that can unhinge the cosmos, and is unleashed upon those persons who deny REVEALED TRUTH.
   - "Heaven" is the INVISIBLE ORIGIN OF THE GEOPOLITICAL FUTURE. Its force is surely felt in the TEMPORALITY IN WHICH MEN LIVE.
   - The behavior of men as individuals, cultures and collectives has been STANDARDIZED BY INVISIBLE REALITY. "Ungodliness" and "unrighteousness" are objectionable to the SPIRITUAL REALITIES.
   - Men in the Temporal Dimension have the capacity to make every attempt to "suppress" the relation between SEEN ➡ and UNSEEN.
   - REVELATION is constantly showered upon the TEMPORAL ORDER by the INVISIBLE DIMENSION.
   - Furthermore, REVELATION carried an unexpected characteristic, it makes SUPERNATURAL TRUTH, impossible to know without REVELATION, to be made "evident"!
   - INVISIBLE REALITY isn't just a different kind of place, rather, it is a DYNAMIC, determinant force!
3. The sociological world of men may and can try to "suppress" this SUPERNATURAL ENLIGHTENMENT but, it's a tough system to defeat because it is alive, persistent, and loaded with creative force!
4. Any denial of ultimate reality has a cost to it! It is the submergence of mankind into TEMPORAL vagaries! In that soup we suffocate and morally die!

Reflecting on 1 Corinthians:

What's the Main Point or Generalization this Lesson makes About Reality in this Book of the Bible?

CHANGEPOINTS

I think I need to change my view of reality to match God's in the following areas:

Make a list here of other verses in the book that deal with God's view of reality

1

2

3

4

5

6

7

8

From 1 Corinthians

THE STRUCTURE OF REALITY.

1. "Paul, called as an apostle of Jesus Christ by the will of God, and Sosthenes our brother", 1:1. The most important factor in TEMPORAL REALITY is "the will of God"; forcing and flexing its determinant powers over human time, life and history!
2. There is a severe DIMENSIONAL DIFFERENCE BETWEEN INVISIBLE ➡ and VISIBLE REALITY. And that puts some people out! "For the word of the cross is foolishness to those who are perishing, but to those who are being saved it is the power of God", 1:18.
3. INVISIBLE REALITY is inimical to human wisdom! "For it is written, I will destroy the wisdom of the wise, and the cleverness of the clever I will set aside", 1:18, 19.
4. Eventually (it's just a matter of time), the wisdom of Marx, Freud, Nietzsche, the postmodernists and other false philosophies will be destroyed and set aside, because they conflict with the Gospel's Truth! They have no future under the regime of INVISIBLE REALITY.
5. The only true ADVANCEMENT in this part of reality is SPIRITUAL! "But God has chosen the foolish things of the world to shame the wise, and God has chosen the weak things of the world to shame the things which are strong, and the base things of the world and the despised God has chosen, the things that are not, so that He may nullify the things that are, so that no man may boast before God", 1:27-29.
6. INVISIBLE REALITY has its own agenda and ways of behavior! There is a LIVING REALITY beyond time, materiality and the human mind. "But we speak God's wisdom in a mystery, the hidden wisdom which God predestined before the ages to our glory", 2:7. Human existence has two possibilities; one is the dead-end of human wisdom and the other is what many consider an alien form of living—one that does not fit with general human history.
7. On that basis the enemies of God crucified the Son of God, 2:8-10. That will never be forgotten by the Almighty!
8. INVISIBLE REALITY is in perpetual conflict with "the flesh", a kind of RADICAL IMMATURITY: "And I, brethren could not speak to you as to spiritual men, but as to men of flesh, as to infants in Christ", 3:1.
9. Men of the flesh are RADICALLY ONE-DIMENSIONAL. The UNSEEN REALITY is of absolutely no concern to them! Neither its promises nor its warnings are heeded, they are lost!

10. The Lord intends to remake the destiny of the Human race in His spiritual mold: "it is sown a natural body, it is raised a spiritual body. If there is a natural body, there is also a spiritual body", 15:44. This is the promise of ETERNAL RENEWAL, by the will of INVISIBLE REALITY.

we can either choose the

REPRESENTATIONS OF GOD

about reality, **about the world,**

about every detail of our lives;

or, we can make our own...

It is that simple.

Meme from Representational Research artist Elizabeth Darnell. For information about terms, see the Glossary at RepresentationalResearch.com.

Reflecting on 2 Corinthians:

What's the Main Point or Generalization this Lesson makes About Reality in this Book of the Bible?

CHANGEPOINTS

I think I need to change my view of reality to match God's in the following areas:

Make a list here of other verses in the book that deal with God's view of reality

1

2

3

4

5

6

7

8

From 2 Corinthians

THE STRUCTURE OF REALITY

1. "For our proud confidence is this: the testimony of our conscience, that in holiness and godly sincerity, not in fleshly wisdom but in the grace of God, we have conducted ourselves in the world, toward you", 1:12.
2. Every believer's life is intended to become an OUTPOST OF INVISIBLE REALITY IN THE LOWER ORDER OF THINGS—where the minds of men so merge with INVISIBLE REALITY that they become one piece!
3. "Who also made us adequate as servants of a new covenant, not of the letter but of the Spirit; for the letter kills, but the Spirit gives life. But if the ministry of death in letters engraved on stones, came with glory, so that the sons of Israel could not look intently at the face of Moses because of the glory of his face, fading as it was, how will the ministry of the Spirit fail to be even more with glory?", 3:6-8.
4. This world cannot afford to be forever chained to the single dimension of TEMPORAL REALITY. Nor can the minds of men here tolerate its limitations and its minimalist scope of comprehension! The sons of Israel tried too often to mire the REVELATION OF GOD IN THE bog of the LOWER ORDER OF REALITY. The mind however has the potential to escape the confines of LETTERISM and ascend to the HIGHER ORDER OF SPIRITUAL INTELLIGENCE THAT IS CALLED FAITH.
5. Built on the analogy of the Holy Spirit, which immediately transcends all things TEMPORAL, so may the mind, heart and soul of a man ascend beyond its surroundings! That is the mystery of SPIRITUALITY.
6. This calls for a comprehensive RENUNCIATION OF THIS WORLD: "Therefore, since we have this ministry, as we received mercy, we do not lose heart, but we have renounced the things hidden because of shame, not walking in craftiness or adulterating the word of God, but by the manifestation of truth, commending ourselves to every man's conscience in the sight of God", 4:1, 2.
7. The idea is to shuck the fleshy nature in favor of that which represents the pure INVISIBLE REALITY. Here is the most profound change of which is capable! Not just an exchange of behavioral patterns, rather a complete transformation of how one grasps REALITY.
8. The proof of this TRANSFORMATION is how one chooses to live, think and behave! "For we know that if the earthly tent which is our house is torn down, we have a building from God, a house not made with

hands, eternal in the heavens", 5:1. How we face the specter of death is proof enough!

9. Christians look for something beyond the mundane: "For indeed in this house we groan, longing to be clothed with our dwelling from heaven", 5:2. Why? "Now He who prepared us for this very purpose is God, who gave to us the Spirit as a pledge", 5:5. We have a down payment, so to speak. And that will accompany us on the long journey through this world, teaching us, whispering to us to remember that "this ain't all that there is"!
10. Here are the RULES FOR THE ROAD: "Therefore, being always of good courage, and knowing that while we are at home in the body we are absent from the Lord—for we walk by faith, not by sight—we are of good courage, I say, and prefer rather to be absent from the body and to be at home with Lord", 5:6-8. So we consequently seek one "value above others—"to be pleasing to Him", 5:9.

The

BIBLE

demands for itself the place of

AGENT

and that we yield our minds to it.

Meme from Representational Research artist Elizabeth Darnell. For information about terms, see the Glossary at RepresentationalResearch.com.

. Reflecting on Galatians:

What's the Main Point or Generalization this Lesson makes About Reality in this Book of the Bible?

CHANGEPOINTS

I think I need to change my view of reality to match God's in the following areas:

Make a list here of other verses in the book that deal with God's view of reality

1

2

3

4

5

6

7

8

From Galatians

THE STRUCTURE OF REALITY

1. The relation of INVISIBLE REALITY ➡ to the VISIBLE SIDE is very well captured here: "Paul, an apostle (not sent from man, but through Jesus Christ and God the Father, who raised Him from the dead)", 1:1. IT IS A RELATION OF PURE POWER.
2. He furthermore behooves believers to pursue the INVISIBLE above anything TEMPORAL. "For am I now seeking the favor of men or of God? Or am I striving to please men? If I were still trying to please men, I would not be a bondservant of Christ", 1:10.
3. There had been a time when Paul did not try to please God! But those days had long passed and he had turned a sincere ear to INVISIBLE REALITY. He did not intend to go back to a false consciousness of REALITY. His perceptions had been widened and deepened! And that by REVELATION.
4. A SUPERNATURAL MEANS OF COMMUNICATING with man had been plugged into the LOWER ORDER OF REALITY. It was inviolate! "For I would have you know, brethren, that the gospel which was preached by me is not according to man. For I neither received it from man, nor was I taught it, but I received it through a revelation of Jesus Christ", 1:11, 12.
5. So, the INVISIBLE REALITY can be known and it can advance its purpose through men in time and materiality!
6. Men in time, living in concert with HIGHER ORDER REALITY, CAN GLORIFY THE INVISIBLE GOD BEHIND REALITY. The personal change in a single man can project the truth of the UNSEEN TO OTHERS: "but only, they kept hearing, 'He who once persecuted us is now preaching the faith which he once tried to destroy'. And they were glorifying God because of me", 1:23, 24.
7. TEMPORAL HIERARCHIES OF IMPORTANCE lost their importance and their advantages evaporated for one so constrained by HIGHER REALITY. "But from those who were of high reputation (what they were makes no difference to me; God shows no partiality)—well, those who were of reputation contributed nothing", 2:6.
8. Paul, in the grip of the ABSOLUTE DIMENSION, WAS UNIMPRESSED WITH HUMAN POSITIONALITY. We must care less about our enemies and their obvious political power!
9. A RADICAL CONCLUSION had been reached by Paul and that conclusion was a message to all believers! "Now those who belong to Christ

Jesus have crucified the flesh with its passions and desires. If we live by the Spirit, let us also walk by the Spirit", 5:24, 25.

10. THE SUPER REALITIES THAT SURROUND US and IN WHICH WE BELIEVE, ARE OUR DETERMINANT CONTEXT and WE, THEREFORE, LIVE ACCORDINGLY.

AGENT -> PATIENT

Word of God -> Mind of Man

active passive

Meme from Representational Research artist Elizabeth Darnell. For information about terms, see the Glossary at RepresentationalResearch.com.

Reflecting on Ephesians:

What's the Main Point or Generalization this Lesson makes About Reality in this Book of the Bible?

CHANGEPOINTS

I think I need to change my view of reality to match God's in the following areas:

Make a list here of other verses in the book that deal with God's view of reality

1

2

3

4

5

6

7

8

From Ephesians

THE STRUCTURE OF REALITY.

1. There is "one God and Father of all who is over all and through all and in all", 4:6.
2. INVISIBLE REALITY is suffused into all of creation and it's difficult to grasp the meaning of that! But the meaning must surely include the absence of any autonomy in the presence of God.
3. The apostle affirms through the use of analogy, that REALITY is hierarchical. "Therefore be imitators of God, as beloved children and walk in love, just as Christ also loved you and gave Himself up for us, an offering and a sacrifice to God as a fragrant aroma", 5:1, 2. This is a remarkable set of words, calling us to imitate the emissary of INVISIBLE REALITY as we live in the daily stream of our temporal existence! There is nothing not taxing about this!
4. Christ came to redeem us and show us the way through the maze of LOWER REALITY. Our place in this hierarchy is precise and exacting!
5. "But immorality or any impurity or greed must not even be named among you, as is proper among saints; and there must be no filthiness and silly talk, or coarse jesting, which are not fitting, but rather giving of thanks", 5:3, 4.
6. The hierarchy between INVISIBLE ➡ and VISIBLE REALITY is the template for certain relations among men. It is the framework for marriage! "Wives be subject to your own husbands, as to the Lord", 5:22. This not "male supremacy", but rather a SUPERNATURAL STRUCTURE FOR THE MARRIAGE BOND!
7. "But as the church is subject to Christ also the wives ought to be to their husbands in everything", 5:24.
8. It is the structure for family life: "Children, obey your parents in the Lord for this is right", 6:1 (it is approved). Here we have the WAY OF THE UNIVERSE.
9. "Slaves, be obedient to those who are your masters according to the flesh, with fear and trembling, in sincerity of your heart, as to Christ", 6:5.
10. Our behavior in these relations are pictures of the GREATER REALITY! That is why success in these relations carried us beyond personal gratification!

Reflecting on Philippians:

What's the Main Point or Generalization this Lesson makes About Reality in this Book of the Bible?

CHANGEPOINTS

I think I need to change my view of reality to match God's in the following areas:

Make a list here of other verses in the book that deal with God's view of reality

1

2

3

4

5

6

7

8

From Philippians

THE STRUCTURE OF REALITY

1. There is a startling TRUTH revealed in this text: PERSONAL CIRCUMSTANCES REGARDLESS OF THEIR NATURE ARE PUT AT THE DISPOSAL OF THE INVISIBLE REALITY.
2. The apostle had been arrested and imprisoned in Philippi but, "Now I want you to know, brethren, that my circumstances have turned out for the greater progress of the gospel", 1:12.
3. He perhaps was not delighted with the distress of his circumstance, yet the apostle could rejoice in a very large and immediate benefit to the purpose of God!
4. Paul had been, in his own words, "... appointed for the defense of the gospel", 1:16. Since he had been so appointed, then his personal circumstances had also been appointed for the same defense of the gospel.
5. Circumstances, under conditions imposed by INVISIBLE REALITY, would not materialize inadvertently not casually!
6. Paul's body was equally put at the disposal of the Almighty! That case carried certain risks: however, "according to my earnest expectation and hope, that I will not be put to shame in anything, but that with all boldness, Christ will even now, as always, be exalted in my body, whether by life or by death", 1:20.
7. The writer demonstrates a certain transitional necessity: from persecutor of the church ➡ to a committed exponent of the gospel necessitates what we may refer to as METAPHYSICAL CONCLUSIONS— Paul understood that his personal circumstances were the result of ABSOLUTE MEANING. God was part of his experience! And that produced consequences with real time effects!
8. It is possible to espouse belief in the gospel and yet comprehend personal experience as fully separate from it, the result of coincidence or everyday pressures. In which case, THE INVISIBLE REALITY IS EJECTED FROM PERSONAL CONDITIONS and circumstances!
9. There was a bottom line in Paul's mind and it was determinant: "For to me to live is Christ and to die is gain", 1:21.
10. The apostle wrote to the believers and put emphasis upon the CONTROL INFLUENCE OF INVISIBLE REALITY UPON THEIR LIVES IN SPACE, TIME and MATERIALITY: "For to you it has been granted for Christ's sake, not only to believe in Him, but also to suffer for His sake, experiencing the same conflict which you saw in me, and hear to be in me", 1:29, 30.

Reflecting on Colossians:

What's the Main Point or Generalization this Lesson makes About Reality in this Book of the Bible?

CHANGEPOINTS

I think I need to change my view of reality to match God's in the following areas:

Make a list here of other verses in the book that deal with God's view of reality

1

2

3

4

5

6

7

8

From Colossians

THE STRUCTURE OF REALITY

1. The REALITY OF GOD and FAITH IN HIM and His REVELATION PULLS THE THREADS OF OUR LIVES TOGETHER.
2. "Since we heard of your faith in Christ Jesus and the love which you have for all the saints; because of the hope laid up for you in heaven, of which you previously heard in the word of truth, the gospel", 1:4, 5.
3. And there is a life beyond this limited range of REALITY of materiality and fleeting time! "...giving thanks to the Father, who has qualified us to share in the inheritance of the saints in Light", 1:12.
4. THE FINAL REALITY FACTOR: "He [Jesus] is the image of the invisible God, the firstborn of all creation", 1:15. Jesus outranks all human beings that were ever born or ever would be! INVISIBLE REALITY has stamped its representation upon that which is seen.
5. DEPENDENT TERMS: "He is before all things, and in Him all things hold together", 1:17. Imagine, even though the Son of God was on earth, still He was holding the universe together by His will to do so! HOW REMARKABLE.
6. IRREVERENT MINDS: "And although you were formerly alienated and hostile in mind, engaged in evil deeds", 1:21. INVISIBLE REALITY has always been interested in the way people in the VISIBLE WORLD reason! WE MAY GENERALIZE FROM THIS THAT THERE IS A WAY OF REASONING THAT CORRESPONDS TO THE REVEALED STRUCTURE OF REALITY: A way of reasoning not hostile to the actual relation between God ➡ and time/materiality!
7. The true STRUCTURE OF REALITY is the font of SPIRITUAL MOTIVATION, "Now I rejoice in my sufferings for your sake, and in my flesh I do my share on behalf of His body, which is the church, in filling up what is lacking in Christ's afflictions", 1:24.
8. About the present age: "See to it that no one takes you captive through philosophy and empty deception, according to the tradition of men, according to the elementary principles of the world, rather than according to Christ", 2:8.
9. Today we are inundated with several forms of false philosophies and soul-destroying ideologies! All of which have one source: A FALSE CONCEPTION OF REALITY.
10. Belief in Christ foments a kind of hostility to the elementary principles of the world, lived out in the serial experiences of temporal existence:

"If you have died with Christ to the elementary principles of the world, why, as if you were living in the world, do you submit yourself to decrees such as, 'Do not handle, do not taste, do not touch!", 2:20, 21.

11. What is in our heads matters greatly!

Reflecting on 1 Thessalonians:

What's the Main Point or Generalization this Lesson makes About Reality in this Book of the Bible?

CHANGEPOINTS

I think I need to change my view of reality to match God's in the following areas:

Make a list here of other verses in the book that deal with God's view of reality

1

2

3

4

5

6

7

8

From 1 Thessalonians

THE STRUCTURE OF REALITY

1. Life is to be crafted into the profile of the personages of The INVISIBLE REALITY. "You also became imitators of us and of the Lord, having received the word in much tribulation with the joy of the Holy Spirit", 1:6.
2. This tells us that VISIBLE REALITY is tethered to the INVISIBLE REALITY by indissoluble bonds of the word of God and believing hearts, so ordered!
3. SPIRITUAL LIFE in the sociological world becomes a bit taxing and dangerous: "but after we had already suffered and been mistreated in Philippi, as you know, we had the boldness in our God to speak to you the gospel of God amid much opposition", 2:2.
4. For us, this world is a place and time where courage, conviction and responsibility overreach self-protection, "You are witnesses, and so is God, how devoutly and uprightly and blamelessly we behaved toward you believers; just as you know how we were exhorting and encouraging and imploring each one of you as a father would his own children", 2:10, 11.
5. The most valuable condition in time and materiality is the SPIRITUAL CONDITION OF FAITH, 3:5-8. "For now we really live if you stand firm in the Lord", 3:8.
6. The universe is not ANTINOMIAN (lawless) in character (there is Law here and it will be enforced!) "For this is the will of God, your sanctification; that is, that you abstain from sexual immorality", 4:3. Personal pleasure is not the organizing principle of VISIBLE REALITY. "…that each of you know how to possess his own vessel in sanctification and honor, not in lustful passion, like the Gentiles who do not know God; and that no man transgress and defraud his brother in the matter because the Lord is the avenger in all these things, just as we also told you before and solemnly warned you. For God has not called us for the purpose of impurity, but in sanctification. So he who rejects this is not rejecting man but the God who gives His Holy Spirit to you", 4:4-8.
7. The phenomenon of death is not the end of anything! It is, in fact, the beginning!, 4:13-18.
8. Believers must dissent from the world cultures! Some thinkers have gone on the record, espousing that it is impossible for anyone to escape the gravity of one's native culture!
9. The answer is in dissent! The writer Rod Dreher suggests that believers not participate in certain cultural practices. We read of these in 5:12-28.

Reflecting on 2 Thessalonians:

What's the Main Point or Generalization this Lesson makes About Reality in this Book of the Bible?

CHANGEPOINTS

I think I need to change my view of reality to match God's in the following areas:

Make a list here of other verses in the book that deal with God's view of reality

1

2

3

4

5

6

7

8

From 2 Thessalonians

THE STRUCTURE OF REALITY

1. Somewhat shocking: the judgment of God is an active participant in human affairs! "This is a plain indication of God's righteous judgment so that you will be considered worthy of the kingdom of God, for which indeed you are suffering", 1:5.
2. The church is a COSMIC STRUCTURE, "For after all it is only just for God to repay with affliction those who afflict you, and to give relief to you who are afflicted and to us as well when the Lord Jesus will be revealed from heaven with His mighty angels in flaming fire", 1:6, 7.
3. The church is not a mundane organization. nor a mere loose association of believers! Quite the contrary, it is directly shepherded by the Almighty Himself and He can be very avenging toward those of the world who willfully afflict and assault believers!
4. God is involved in this world and intimately! Think China, North Korea, for example!
5. There is a REALITY called "eternal destruction", 1:9. It has no natural explanation. Certain people who engage in these anti-God pursuits will be sent "away from the presence of the Lord and from the glory of His power", 1:9.
6. VISIBLE REALITY exists in the shadow of a fearsome force, which is INVISIBLE REALITY. It is active, observant and mindful of every believer who suffers for the cause of SPIRITUAL HIGHER ORDER REALITY.
7. Every believer is a vessel of INVISIBLE REALITY, "so that the name of our Lord Jesus will be glorified in you, and you in Him, according to the grace of our God and the Lord Jesus Christ", 1:12.
8. Because of the relation between VISIBLE ➡ and INVISIBLE REALITY, then. "… not be quickly shaken from your composure or be disturbed either by a spirit or a message or a letter as if from us, to the effect that the day of the Lord has come", 2:2.
9. According to the STRUCTURE OF REALITY, no one should dare "oppose and exalt himself above every so-called god or object of worship, so that he takes his seat in the temple of God, displaying himself as being God", 2:4.
10. Such people are in league with Satan, 2:9. Including governments and social institutions! Instead we pursue INVISIBLE REALITY, and so, "May the Lord direct your hearts into the love of God and into the steadfastness of Christ", 3:5.

Reflecting on 1 Timothy:

What's the Main Point or Generalization this Lesson makes About Reality in this Book of the Bible?

CHANGEPOINTS

I think I need to change my view of reality to match God's in the following areas:

Make a list here of other verses in the book that deal with God's view of reality

1

2

3

4

5

6

7

8

From 1 Timothy

THE STRUCTURE OF REALITY

1. From the apostle's position within time and materiality, he calls out to INVISIBLE REALITY, "Now to the King eternal, immortal, invisible, the only God, be honor and glory forever and ever. Amen", 1:17.
2. The writer makes appeal to ULTIMATE CAUSATION, 2:1-4. Causation is not principally a TEMPORAL PHENOMENON. It is, in fact, a SPIRITUAL REALITY. Which REALITY TRANSCENDS WHAT ARE CALLED THE LAWS OF NATURE.
3. People are called to respond to ULTIMATE REALITY in demonstrable ways! "Likewise I want women to adorn themselves with proper clothing, modestly and discreetly, not with braided hair and gold and pearls or costly garments, but rather by means of good works, as is proper for women making a claim to godliness", 2:9, 10.
4. This is a kind of consonant reaction to HIGHER ORDER REALITY. In the SPIRITUAL ORDER as contained in scripture, the relation between the genders is analogical to the relation between INVISIBLE ➡ and VISIBLE REALITY. "But I do not allow a woman to teach or exercise authority over a man, but to remain quiet. For it was Adam who created and then Eve. And it was not Adam who was deceived, but the woman being deceived, fell into transgression", 2:12-14.
5. Therefore believers must never take the origin of the VISIBLE DIMENSION for granted.
6. Believers, individually and the collective of the church are to appreciate "how one ought to conduct himself in the household of God, which is the church of the living God, the pillar and support of the truth", 3:15.
7. It is INVISIBLE REALITY that draws the lines by which men are to contemplate their place in time and space. "But godliness actually is a means of great gain when accompanied by contentment. For we have brought nothing into the world, so we cannot take anything out of it either. If we have food and covering with these we shall be content. But those who want to get rich fall into temptation and a snare and many foolish and harmful desires which plunge men into ruin and destruction", 6:6-9.
8. The STRUCTURE OF REALITY determines what right perception and behavior is!
9. This REVEALED PERCEPTION ADMONISHES ALL BELIEVERS: "…the love of money is a root of all sorts of evil, and some by longing for it

have wandered away from the faith and pierced themselves with many griefs… flee from these things, you man of God, and pursue righteousness, godliness, faith, love, perseverance and gentleness… Fight the good fight of faith, take hold of the eternal life to which you were called, and you made the good confession in the presence of many witnesses", 6:10-12.

10. VISIBLE REALITY is not the full picture of REALITY. This is a FUNDAMENTAL TRUTH.

Reflecting on 2 Timothy:

What's the Main Point or Generalization this Lesson makes About Reality in this Book of the Bible?

CHANGEPOINTS

I think I need to change my view of reality to match God's in the following areas:

Make a list here of other verses in the book that deal with God's view of reality

1

2

3

4

5

6

7

8

From 2 Timothy

THE STRUCTURE OF REALITY

1. "Be diligent to present yourself approved to God as a workman who does not need to be ashamed, accurately handling the word of truth", 2:15.
2. The apostle affirms the ACTUALITY OF GOD, the possible relation with Him, and that of REVELATION.
3. "Nevertheless, the firm foundation of God stands, having this seal, 'The Lord knows those who are His,' and, 'Everyone who names the name of the Lord is to abstain from wickedness'", 2:19. Because of the nature of the TRUE GOD, then, the universe is a MORAL UNIVERSE.
4. Under the authority of the existent God, human behavior is to be a consequence of the STRUCTURE OF REALITY. "...with gentleness correcting those who are in opposition, if perhaps God may grant them repentance leading to the knowledge of the truth", 2:25.
5. Individuals can effectively shape themselves into an isomorphic form of the will of God! Nothing, therefore, has to be the way that it is!
6. Anyone can rise above animal instincts to approximate the character of INVISIBLE REALITY. In this kind of universe, God is not the problem! Mankind is the problem. "But realize this, that in the last days difficult times will come", 3:1. There is a reason for all that trouble: No one will respect the sovereignty of the God of creation. "For men will be lovers of self, lovers of money, boastful, arrogant, revilers, disobedient to parents, ungrateful, unholy, unloving, irreconcilable, malicious gossips, without self-control, brutal, haters of good, treacherous, reckless, conceited, lovers of pleasure rather lovers of God", 3:2-4.
7. Such men are delusional, thinking themselves to be God!
8. No longer part of creation, they are the creators. They became religious but unbelievers, 3:5.
9. These people love this world and have no preference for INVISIBLE REALITY. But PERSONAL TRANSFORMATION CAN BE HAD. SUPERNATURAL PROVISIONS have been made! "All Scripture is inspired by God and profitable for teaching, for reproof, for correction, for training in righteousness; so that the man of God may be adequate, equipped for every good deed", 3:16, 17.
10. Think of it! Here are the means to reshape and redeem the nature of fallen men. This is quite revolutionary! This invalidates all human philosophical quests for PROGRESS! Outside of God there is no other true possibility for what they seek! Socialism as the precursor of communism and other collectivists schemes cannot do the job!

Reflecting on 2 Timothy (part 2):

What's the Main Point or Generalization this Lesson makes About Reality in this Book of the Bible?

CHANGEPOINTS

I think I need to change my view of reality to match God's in the following areas:

Make a list here of other verses in the book that deal with God's view of reality

1

2

3

4

5

6

7

8

From 2 Timothy (part two)

THE STRUCTURE OF REALITY

RULES FOR THE WORLD—THIS LEADS TO RECOVERY, REDEMPTION AND STABILITY.

1. DO NOT BE ASHAMED OF THE CHRISTIAN RELIGION, 1:8.
2. REMEMBER: THE REAL NATIONAL TREASURE IS THE RELATION A NATION HAS TO GOD, 1:13-18.
3. IMPORTANCE DOES NOT END WITH THE AFFAIRS OF DAILY LIFE, 2:1-7.
4. THERE IS A FAULTLESS ETERNAL STANDARD STANDING BEHIND THE MATERIAL and SOCIAL WORLDS, 2:8-13.
5. DO NOT INDULGE IN "WORD GAMES", 3:14-19.
6. .DO NOT CATER TO THE YOUTH OF THE NATION, 2:20-26.
7. SELF-GRATIFICATION LEADS TO NATIONAL and SOCIETAL COLLAPSE, 3:1-7.
8. SOCIAL DISINTEGRATION IS A PERNICIOUS EVIL, 3:10-17.
9. THE PRESENCE OF GOD IS AN HISTORICAL FACTOR, 4:1-8.
10. OPPOSITION TO THE WORD OF GOD IS UNAVOIDABLE, 4:16-19.
11. THE SACRED LANGUAGE MANIFOLD OFFERS MORE THAN JUST COMFORT TO BELIEVERS and CHURCHES, IT IS A MESSAGE FROM HIGHER REALITY and IT DEALS WITH RULES GOVERNING NATIONAL EXPERIENCE.

Reflecting on Titus:

What's the Main Point or Generalization this Lesson makes About Reality in this Book of the Bible?

CHANGEPOINTS

I think I need to change my view of reality to match God's in the following areas:

Make a list here of other verses in the book that deal with God's view of reality

1

2

3

4

5

6

7

8

From Titus

THE STRUCTURE OF REALITY

1. "Paul, a bond-servant of God and an apostle of Jesus Christ, for the faith of those chosen of God and the knowledge of the truth which is according to godliness, in the hope of eternal life, which God, who cannot lie, promised long ages ago, but at the proper time manifested, even His word, in the proclamation with which I was entrusted according to the commandment of God our Savior, to Titus, my true child in a common faith: Grace and peace from the Father and Christ Jesus our Savior", 1:1-4.
2. This "introduction" is brimming with the nature of the STRUCTURE OF REALITY.
3. Under the authority of THE INVISIBLE REALITY, certain people are chosen and charged with the obligation to promote the will and purpose of God. Paul was one of those.
4. "Faith" is the index chosen by God to link the INVISIBLE ➡ to the VISIBLE!
5. The will of God has chosen those of His selection to be blessed with a relation to Him.
6. "Eternal life" is successor to temporal existence and that, promised by the Almighty Himself to the faithful!
7. The Creator of all REALITY IS THE PERSONAGE who does not lie.
8. On His own initiative God makes promises that are absolute and far reaching to mortal men and by them, He clarifies the future of those who believe!
9. Time is modulated, orchestrated and coordinated by the power and purpose of HIGHER ORDER REALITY.
10. The "commandments" of God are determinant!
11. There is no question, whatsoever, that THE VISIBLE DIMENSION OF REALITY is purely subordinate to the UNSEEN REALITY.
12. TEMPORAL REALITY is not permanent, by any means, it is the gift of a world unseen! "Instructing us to deny ungodliness and worldly desires and to live sensibly, righteously and godly in the present age, looking for the blessed hope and the appearing of the glory of our great God and Savior, Christ Jesus", 2:12, 13.
13. THIS WORLD IS A ONE-WAY TRIP.

Reflecting on Philemon:

What's the Main Point or Generalization this Lesson makes About Reality in this Book of the Bible?

CHANGEPOINTS

I think I need to change my view of reality to match God's in the following areas:

Make a list here of other verses in the book that deal with God's view of reality

1

2

3

4

5

6

7

8

From Philemon

THE STRUCTURE OF REALITY

1. "Therefore, I have enough confidence in Christ to order you to do what is proper", V.8.
2. The apostle's point is that the STRUCTURE OF REALITY is the controlling context for determining what is "proper" for believers to do. In the issue of this book, slavery, the proper thing to do is dispense with that artificial relationship!
3. Onesimus was a legal slave of Philemon. Onesimus ran away, leaving his employer and master. Eventually, he joined Paul and the apostle taught Onesimus the gospel. As he rose up out of the water of baptism a new question surfaced.
4. Philemon had been previously made a Christian and then Onesimus became a believer in Christ. So what does that coequality do to the institution of slavery under the REVEALED STRUCTURE OF REALITY?
5. Answer: It effectively abolishes slavery as a valid approved relationship between people in the Kingdom of God!
6. If two men, a slave owner and a slave both turn to Christ and are therefore elevated to shared brotherhood, then, slavery cannot apply!
7. That was "proper" for Philemon to observe. At that point both Philemon and Onesimus had the same Master and that was the Almighty! V. 10-16.
8. Previous habits of perception had to therefore, be pushed away as no longer meaningful!
9. Everything had indeed been made new! The STRUCTURE OF REALITY AS BIBLICALLY REVEALED HAD REDEFINED "proper" reasoning and behavior!
10. All things among men had to be reconfigured!

Reflecting on Hebrews:

What's the Main Point or Generalization this Lesson makes About Reality in this Book of the Bible?

CHANGEPOINTS

I think I need to change my view of reality to match God's in the following areas:

Make a list here of other verses in the book that deal with God's view of reality

1

2

3

4

5

6

7

8

From Hebrews

THE STRUCTURE OF REALITY

1. "God, after He spoke long ago to the fathers in the prophets in many portions and in many ways", 1:1. INVISIBLE REALITY HAD inaugurated a regimen of communicating with men in space and time. One may conclude that men cannot live without the benefit of the knowledge of the SUPERNATURAL MIND and its depth of knowledge and reach of wisdom. It is one of the necessities of life!
2. "In these last days has spoken to us in His Son, whom He appointed heir of all things, through whom also He made the world", 1:2. Again we are cautioned not to believe that time has any NATURALISTIC EXPLANATION OR FONT WHATSOEVER.
3. This is a SUPERNATURAL OUTCOME generated by ABSOLUTE yet INVISIBLE REALITY.
4. "And He is the radiance of His glory and the exact representation of His nature, and upholds all things by the word of His power. When He had made purification of sins, He sat down at the right hand of the majesty on high", 1:3.
5. Jesus came to earth as its source and its Creator! Even now His power is the TRUE STRONG FORCE holding the universe together as one piece! The discipline of physics deals only with artificial aspects of the NATURAL ORDER.
6. Beyond that, Jesus cured the oldest pathology of men: HUMAN SIN, requiring the power of administered "purification" through His death, burial and resurrection! He did that in His flesh!
7. Therefore, REALITY is again shown to be a hierarchy with Christ shown to be at the top of that structure! And He is qualitatively better than anyone who has ever lived or ever will live, 1:4.
8. The STRUCTURE OF REALITY is a FIELD OF COMMUNICATION and it is a universe governed by SUPERNATURAL CHARACTER: "You have loved righteousness and hated lawlessness", 1:9.
9. The Son of God is the undisputed Master of this world and He "sits at My right hand, until I make Your enemies a footstool for Your feet", 1:13.
10. God ordained a Covenant to link God ➡ to men in the lower dimension. According to Genesis 17, the original covenant was presented as THE SPIRITUAL ENGINE THAT GENERATED THE FUTURE. One may imagine the reach of "the new and better Covenant!" Both Covenants pushed NATURALISM to the margins of history and pushed NATURE out of Causation!

11. "… by faith we understand that the worlds were prepared by the word of God, so that what is seen was not made out of things which are visible", 11:3. Extraordinary!

Reflecting on James:

What's the Main Point or Generalization this Lesson makes About Reality in this Book of the Bible?

CHANGEPOINTS

I think I need to change my view of reality to match God's in the following areas:

Make a list here of other verses in the book that deal with God's view of reality

1

2

3

4

5

6

7

8

From James

THE STRUCTURE OF REALITY

1. "But if any of you lack wisdom, let him ask of God, who gives to all generously and without reproach, and it will be given to him", 1:5.
2. The source of superior wisdom, transcending human wisdom, is HIGHER ORDER REALITY. Man can go beyond his limitations! People should aspire to HIGHER ORDER UNDERSTANDING. The temporal order is governed and regulated by UNSEEN REALITY.
3. "If anyone thinks himself to be religious, and yet does not bridle his tongue but deceives his own heart, this man's religion is worthless", 1:35.
4. True religion is an obligation before the INVISIBLE REALITY, which is the moral government of the world of men! It must not be tampered with!
5. "Faith" is not minimalist in any sense. "You believe that God is one. You do well; the demons also believe and shudder", 2:19. The demons acknowledge that God is there and that He is powerful, still, those beings have no intention of existing on the standard of behavior revealed to mankind in Scripture! "But are you willing to recognize, you foolish fellow, that faith without works is useless", 2:20.
6. Biblical faith is a form of behavior in the lower dimension of reality. It does not consist of just doctrinal adherence (it is a plenary form of life!)
7. Faith garners the approval of God and that has a great deal to do with subsequent life of believers!
8. "Prayer" is proof of faith above human lived experience, 5:13-15.
9. The prophet "Elijah" is the proof personage of this truth! "Elijah was a man with a nature like ours, and he prayed earnestly that it would not rain… it did not rain on the earth for three years and six months. Then he prayed again, and the sky poured rain and the earth produced its fruit", 5:17, 18. However, the VISIBLE PART OF REALITY is NOT A PERMANENT REALITY. It is transient.
10. "You too be patient; strengthen your hearts, for the coming of the Lord is near", 5:8. We believers are the only things that will survive His coming!

Reflecting on 1 Peter:

What's the Main Point or Generalization this Lesson makes About Reality in this Book of the Bible?

CHANGEPOINTS

I think I need to change my view of reality to match God's in the following areas:

Make a list here of other verses in the book that deal with God's view of reality

1 ______

2 ______

3 ______

4 ______

5 ______

6 ______

7 ______

8 ______

From 1 Peter

THE STRUCTURE OF REALITY

1. The VISIBLE REALITY is the PROVING GROUND of personal faith! Not a playground for human concupiscence!
2. That particular meaning was imposed upon the full range of human personal experience!
3. ". . who are protected by the power of God through faith for a salvation ready to be revealed in the last time. In this you greatly rejoice, even though now for a little while, if necessary, you have been distressed by various trials, so that the proof of your faith, being more precious than gold which is perishable, even though tested by fire, may be found to result in praise and glory and honor at the revelation of Jesus Christ; and though you have not seen Him, you love Him, and though you do not see Him now, but believe in Him, you greatly rejoice with joy inexpressible and full of glory", 1:5-8.
4. The Almighty has set down the governing truths for SPIRITUAL EXISTENCE IN THE TEMPORAL SETTING.
5. And the Lord Himself had determined in His mind that true faith is the most precious commodity on the face of the earth! Nothing else compares with its value! It can buy something that gold itself and lots of it could never provide: THE APPROBATION OF GOD HIMSELF.
6. "distress" is the NECESSARY PATH to PROVEN FAITH. There is PROVEN FAITH and then there is a kind of faith that doesn't ever "get in the ring"!
7. Well, we are under the gun, whether we are comfortable with it or not! But Peter presents that entire POTENTIAL EXPERIENCE as a very positive circumstance! Yes, our distresses are a GOOD THING in the economy of INVISIBLE REALITY.
8. The apostle instructs us to "rejoice" in those historical conditions! Finally, such pressures end in "praise", "glory" and "honor". How improbable!
9. There is no doubt that PROVEN FAITH carries the believing mind much beyond the confines of human intelligence!
10. We are suspended in the REALITY OF GOD.

Reflecting on 2 Peter:

What's the Main Point or Generalization this Lesson makes About Reality in this Book of the Bible?

CHANGEPOINTS

I think I need to change my view of reality to match God's in the following areas:

Make a list here of other verses in the book that deal with God's view of reality

1

2

3

4

5

6

7

8

From 2 Peter

THE STRUCTURE OF REALITY

1. Access has been granted to the believers who seek a closer association with INVISIBLE REALITY: "For by these He has granted to us His precious and magnificent promises, so that by them you may become partakers of the divine nature, having escaped the corruption that is in the world by lust", 1:4.
2. Men, in time and materiality, that is, the LOWER ORDER OF REALITY, can take on something of the "divine nature" and that shows up in the phenomenon of personal behavior!
3. Believing that temporal reality is the true context of man, essentially, veils the mind to the GREATER REALITY: "For if these qualities are yours and are increasing, they render you neither useless nor unfruitful in the true knowledge of our Lord Jesus Christ", 1:8.
4. This temporal dimension cannot discover on its own the HIGHER ORDER OF REALITY.
5. There is a governing priority: "... entrance into the eternal kingdom of our Lord and Savior Jesus Christ will be abundantly supplied to you", 1:11.
6. The FLOOD WARNING: "For God... did not spare the ancient world, but preserved Noah, a preacher of righteousness, with seven others, when He brought a flood upon the world of the ungodly", 2:4, 5. The ungodly rebelled against HIGHER ORDER REALITY and were utterly destroyed!
7. The DESTRUCTION WARNING: "and if He condemned the cities of Sodom and Gomorrah to destruction by reducing them to ashes, having made them an example to those who would live ungodly lives thereafter", 2:6. The cities of the plain were annihilated by the personal and direct action of God, therefore, one must respect fully the RELATION BETWEEN THE THREE DIMENSIONS OF REALITY.
8. PROOF OF PROPOSITION: "...then the Lord knows how to rescue the godly from temptation, and to keep the unrighteousness under punishment for the day of judgment, and especially those who indulge the flesh in its corrupt desires and despise authority", 2:8, 9.
9. Outcomes, here, are ultimate! It's either rescue or judgment. This dimension fools the eye, it is from the LOWER DIMENSION OF REALITY that we need rescue! So this dimension is not all that there is. There is another dimension HIGHER and PERMANENT that holds the promise of eternal life and not this world!

10. Any other comprehension of REALITY is insufficient, false and dangerous! Believers are not permitted to concede their lives to LOWER REALITY. To do that is to be subhuman. "But these, like unreasoning animals, born as creatures of instinct to be captured and killed, reviling where they have no knowledge, will in the destruction of those creatures also be destroyed", 2:12.
11. We proclaim and warn and exhort, some give heed and some will not, but that does not impede the coming resolution of TEMPORAL EXISTENCE.

Reflecting on 1 John:

What's the Main Point or Generalization this Lesson makes About Reality in this Book of the Bible?

CHANGEPOINTS

I think I need to change my view of reality to match God's in the following areas:

Make a list here of other verses in the book that deal with God's view of reality

1

2

3

4

5

6

7

8

From 1 John

THE STRUCTURE OF REALITY

1. What was the origin of the Christ? ANSWER: He had no origin, He was the origin: "What was from the beginning, what we have heard, what we have seen with our eyes, what we have looked at and touched with our hands, concerning the word of life", 1:1.
2. Jesus was from the INVISIBLE and ETERNAL DIMENSION OF REALITY. So there was and is an OPEN INDEX relating the INVISIBLE ➡ and THE VISIBLE TOGETHER AS ONE PIECE.
3. Jesus is the record, in His person, of these two dimensions in contact: STRATEGIC CONTACT.
4. Life did not evolve on earth; it was purposeful evidence of the other dimension! "And the life was manifested, and we have seen and testify and proclaim to you the eternal life, which was with the Father and was manifested", 1:2. AND THERE IT IS! The INVISIBLE is manifested in the VISIBLE. That is the relation between the two realms of REALITY.
5. Not only that; a communion has been arranged between the two! "What we have seen and heard we proclaim to you also, so that you too may have fellowship with us; and indeed our fellowship is with the Father, and with His Son Jesus Christ", 1:3.
6. And so the gospel was preached and secures our destiny!
7. The VISIBLE is situated downstream from the "Light"; "God is Light" (1:5-7). The "Light" elucidates the human condition; which is much more than natural, biological and physical; It is SPIRITUAL!
8. Human behavior is correlated to the HIGHER ORDER dimension: "Do not love the world nor the things in the world. If anyone loves the world, the love of the Father is not in Him", 2:15.
9. Those who deny that the INVISIBLE ➡ and the VISIBLE exist and are in contact are characterized as the "antichrist", 2:22-24. THE STRUCTURE OF REALITY demands this form of language!
10. There are, correspondingly, two dimensions of language: "The one who believes in the Son of God has the testimony in himself; the one who does not believe God has made Him a liar, because he has not believed in the testimony that God has given concerning His Son", 5:10.
11. The STRUCTURE OF REALITY has established the rules of the road!

Reflecting on 2 John:

What's the Main Point or Generalization this Lesson makes About Reality in this Book of the Bible?

CHANGEPOINTS

I think I need to change my view of reality to match God's in the following areas:

Make a list here of other verses in the book that deal with God's view of reality

1

2

3

4

5

6

7

8

From 2 John

THE STRUCTURE OF REALITY

1. Revelation is an index (link) between the INVISIBLE ➡ and VISIBLE REALITY. "And this is love, that we walk according to His commandments. This is the commandment, just as you have heard from the beginning, that you should walk in it", V.6.
2. The fact is that VISIBLE REALITY has always been relativized to the INVISIBLE. This arrangement is one of the bottom lines of the Christian religion, and it regulates our understanding of exactly what REALITY is.
3. Therefore, the starting point for contemplation is always the bestowed comprehension of how things are in the universe!
4. "For many deceivers have gone out into the world, those who do not acknowledge Jesus Christ as coming in the flesh. This is the deceiver and the antichrist", V.7.
5. This means, immediately, that human reason and personal experience cannot grasp on its own the true state of affairs! Anyone denying the significance of the REVELATION INDEX is following in the steps of antichrist.
6. Such a person is not a solitary nor singular historical personage. No, it's anyone who decides, in his/her mind to reject the stipulated language about the relative positionality of this world in the big scheme of things.
7. "Watch yourselves, that you do not lose what we have accomplished, but that you may receive a full reward", V.8.
8. Our salvation is quite conditional! No one is permitted to elevate one's self above the authority of Christ! Mankind and trust in its powers of Intellect is nothing less than a form of idolatry!

Reflecting on 3 John:

What's the Main Point or Generalization this Lesson makes About Reality in this Book of the Bible?

CHANGEPOINTS

I think I need to change my view of reality to match God's in the following areas:

Make a list here of other verses in the book that deal with God's view of reality

1

2

3

4

5

6

7

8

From 3 John

THE STRUCTURE OF REALITY

1. A massive line of distinction has been put into TIME and MATERIALITY: "Beloved, do not imitate what is evil, but what is good. The one who does good is of God; the one who does evil has not seen God", V.11.
2. CROSSING THAT LINE OF DEMARCATION HAS VAST MEANING and IMPLICATIONS.
3. Two sources of behavior are available to each of us during our time on earth: (1) THE EXISTENCE OF GOD and His character/nature and (2) The complete absence of God and the irrelevance of the conception of God.
4. All depends upon what one considers to be the ideal.
5. "Imitation" or what is called mimesis is the calculated attempt to PERSONIFY either good or evil.
6. "I wrote something to the church; but Diotrephes, who loves to be first among them, does not accept what we say", V.9.
7. To that man the apostolic word was irrelevant! He simply rejected this line of demarcation.
8. He determined that he would PERSONIFY (embody) the forbidden evil in his dealings and relations with others! Certainly that was a willing pursuit!
9. "Demetrius has received a good testimony from everyone, and from the truth itself; and we add our testimony, and you know that our testimony is true", V.12.
10. Another chose the imitation/personification of good! That also was a conscious pursuit!
11. A person can choose one or the other, but not both! We are called by HIGHER ORDER REALITY to PERSONIFY THE GOOD; which is a function of that HIGHER ORDER. This line of demarcation does not permit concessions to evil, nor conformity to it! So we function in all circumstances on the premise to do good or evil.
12. This rule is given to us by REVELATION and is therefore outside of and beyond man! More than that, it really is a functional solution to many problems! Evil tends toward a cascade of consequences that resolve nothing! Choose the good!

Reflecting on Jude:

What's the Main Point or Generalization this Lesson makes About Reality in this Book of the Bible?

CHANGEPOINTS

I think I need to change my view of reality to match God's in the following areas:

Make a list here of other verses in the book that deal with God's view of reality

1

2

3

4

5

6

7

8

From Jude

THE STRUCTURE OF REALITY

1. "It was also about these men that Enoch, in the seventh generation from Adam, prophesied, saying, 'Behold the Lord came with many thousands of His holy ones, to execute judgment upon all, and to convict all the ungodly of all their ungodly deeds which they have done in an ungodly way, and of all the harsh things which ungodly sinners have spoken against Him", V.14 15.
2. These verses indelibly present the relation between HIGHER ORDER REALITY ➡ and THE LOWER ORDER: COMPLETE DOMINANCE.
3. This coming of the Lord is announced IN ADVANCE TO WARN OF ETERNAL RETRIBUTION BROUGHT TO BEAR UPON UNGODLY PEOPLE IN TIME and MATERIALITY.
4. Against those who reject Christ, in or out of the church, no sin is forgotten. The integrity of the character of SUPERNATURAL REALITY will be demonstrated and upheld! None will escape.
5. None have ever escaped: (1) Not the angels who rebelled, v.6, (2) Not Sodom and Gomorrah, v.7, (3) Not men who defile the flesh, reject authority and revile angelic majesties, v.8 and (4) Not those who appear to be believers but impede the work of Christ, v.12, 13.
6. Jude intends to somewhat brusquely insist that the INVISIBLE REALITY means business!
7. Enoch tells us that what the Lord has planned in its finality has already happened in His eternal mind, V.14.
8. There is nothing abstract about the language of Jude.
9. The Lord does not forget improper language, (v.15). Such language is the attempt to reduce HIGHER ORDER REALITY to the level of the LOWER ORDER.
10. That will not do! "These are grumblers, finding fault, following after their own lusts; they speak arrogantly, flattering people for the sake of gaining an advantage", V.16.
11. INTEGRITY OF SOUL and CHARACTER IS OF THE UTMOST IMPORTANCE.
12. Thus the frontier of the church is protected! INVISIBLE REALITY is ever watchful over the LOWER ORDER.

Reflecting on Revelation:

What's the Main Point or Generalization this Lesson makes About Reality in this Book of the Bible?

CHANGEPOINTS

I think I need to change my view of reality to match God's in the following areas:

Make a list here of other verses in the book that deal with God's view of reality

1

2

3

4

5

6

7

8

From Revelation
THE STRUCTURE OF REALITY

1. "The Revelation of Jesus Christ, which God gave Him to show to His bond-servants, the things which must soon take place; and He sent and communicated it by His angel to His bond-servant John", 1:1.
2. There is an OBJECTIVE INDEX that links the HIGHER ➡ and LOWER ORDERS OF REALITY.
3. God the Father ➡ informed Jesus of forthcoming events ➡ and Jesus instructed His angel ➡ which angel brought the word to John, in the Island of Patmos. This was a CONTINUUM OF OBJECTIVE TRUTH OR WHAT TODAY IS OFTEN REFERRED TO AS A META-NARRATIVE.
4. And that is a NARRATIVE controlling the architecture of future circumstances!
5. HIGHER REALITY HAS TURNED EACH and every believer into a "bond-servant". He/she has no choice in the matter!
6. In addition, there is NO EQUALITY between the two dimensions of REALITY! "I am the Alpha and the Omega, says the Lord God, who is and who was and who is to come, the Almighty", 1:8.
7. John was confronted without warning by One with whom he had to deal! And that One was in no mood to dicker over policy!
8. John was imprisoned because of "the word of God", 1:9. So circumstances and historical conditions were beyond his influence!
9. Bond-servants have no rights, the Almighty does not negotiate with His servants! HISTORY HAPPENS TO THEM.
10. And HISTORY IS about to smack the believers in Asia Minor, where it hurts!
11. The Lord said to John, "Write in a book what you see, and send it to the seven churches: to Ephesus and to Smyrna and to Pergamum and to Thyatira and to Sardis and to Philadelphia and to Laodicea", 1:11. The PERMISSIVE WILL OF GOD will allow those churches to be lashed by persecution! Therefore, there is a working index between the MIND OF GOD ➡ and the letter (the Book of Revelation) sent to the seven churches!
12. "I was in the Spirit on the Lord's day and I heard behind me a loud voice like the sound of a trumpet", 1:10.
13. John turned to see what was behind all of that (1:12-16) and what he saw dropped his blood pressure to nothing. "When I saw Him, I fell at His feet like a dead man. And He placed His right hand on me, saying,

'Do not be afraid; I am the first and the last, and the living One; and I was dead, and behold, I am alive for evermore, and I have the keys of death and of Hades'", 1:17, 18.

AND THAT IS THE STRUCTURE OF REALITY.

Reflections on Conclusion to Series:

NOTES

CONCLUSION TO SERIES – From James 4:7, 8

THE STRUCTURE OF REALITY

1. "Submit therefore to God. Resist the devil and he will flee from you. Draw near to God and He will draw near to you, Cleanse your hands, you sinners; and purify your hearts, you double-minded", 4:7, 8.
2. The subject investigated here is that of EXCLUSIVITY. The claims that God makes upon as believers, are exclusive!
3. There is a truth regarding the devil, who actually exists. He has no wish to waste time and effort! So if you determine in your heart to "resist" his influence, then he will flee from you to pursue more fertile grounds for his purposes!
4. We are additionally taught that double-mindedness constitutes a SPIRITUAL CONDITION CATEGORIZED AS IMPURITY! This surely applies to the structure of reality!
5. Those who come to Christ are not permitted to entertain two opposing perceptions of REALITY. For example, trying to live by (1) A NATURALISTIC/RATIONALISTIC COMPREHENSION OF REALITY, on the one hand and (2) REVEALED UNDERSTANDING OF REALITY, on the other, exemplifies AN IMPURITY OF HEART, MIND and SOUL.
6. This MENTAL STATE OF IMPURITY constantly challenges the integrity of the word of God and consequently, faith!
7. Throughout Scripture, the true axis of faith is one's fidelity to the REVEALED STRUCTURE OF REALITY. That means clearing up the MENTAL IMPURITY OF DOUBLE-MINDEDNESS.
8. Believers shouldn't go through life in constant combat between NATURALISM/RATIONALISM ➡ and REVELATION. Israel of Old was never fully convicted of the truth and efficacy of the REVEALED STRUCTURE OF REALITY.
9. Drawing near to God is the only real antidote to double-mindedness! In other words, one must "cast the die" (make a choice). It's either REVELATION or RELIANCE UPON HUMAN WISDOM and EXPERIENCE. That attempted equilibrium between two diametrically opposed ideas is intolerable to God and insufferable to its holder! It's just too hard to do!
10. We, as believers, are regularly vexed by irritating contradictions! But we must banish double-minded impurity and stand finally, with the Lord and HIS WORD!
11. So the command is to "RESIST THE DEVIL and "DRAW NEAR TO GOD"! This is the pursuit or strategy, if you choose, of EXCLUSIVITY.

Try your hand at generalizing

Choose one of the scripture passages that you found on your own which speaks about reality.

Remember, a generalization is parallel language to the scripture passage but not just a rewording of it. It is extracting a truth from it that is faithful to the meaning of the passage in question, and that is true all throughout the Bible

EXAMPLES:

The story of Goliath and David shows that "material circumstances don't determine outcomes" (Strawn)

"God alone is the author of life in His time and for His purpose" – from the opening and closing of Rachel and Leah's wombs in Genesis 30, Rebekah's womb in Genesis 25, and Sarah's womb in Genesis 21 (Elizabeth Darnell)

"Prayer affects heaven" or another way to say it is "Asking links heaven into my life." I live in direct contact with a material world but faith deals with these circumstances through prayer because I trust God takes direct action on my temporal events. So prayer and trust are tightly knit. James 5: 13-15 is strong evidence for this generalization and I like Psalm 116. Particular verses: I love the Lord, for He has heard my voice, my supplications. verses 1-2, and verse 10 "I believed in you, so I said....." Parallel to this is John 14: 12-14. You can ask for the same works of Jesus like healing, love, acceptance and compassion and have the confidence he will do it! (Jeannie Pace)

NOW, YOUR TURN:

MY GENERALIZATIONS FROM PASSAGES OF SCRIPTURE I FOUND:

NOW, YOUR TURN:

MY GENERALIZATIONS FROM PASSAGES OF SCRIPTURE I FOUND:

NOW, YOUR TURN:

MY GENERALIZATIONS FROM PASSAGES OF SCRIPTURE I FOUND:

Supplemental material

See below how one of Dr. Strawn's more advanced students Jeannie Pace has taken a Strawn concept, The Phases of Faith, and used it to generalize from the book of Habakkuk. This first chart demonstrates the general principles of the Phases of Faith and the second one shows scriptural examples of each phase. Pace then generalizes about those phases in Habakkuk.

phases of faith

God's Word (promise) is backed by His power, oath and character which ends (resolution) all contradictions,

1 | Promise	2 | Contradiction	3 | Resolution
The Word of God represented to us in the Bible in the form of: *command or promise *covenant & God's attributes *prophecy *symbols *our status as heirs	Testing or waiting phase when the promise seems unlikely or unreasonable because of: *time *human logic *physiology *fear *my will	Phase 1 is fulfilled as a result of God's actions Galatians 6:9 we receive a harvest of blessing if we do not give up.

phases of faith in Habakkuk

God's Word (promise) is backed by his oath and character which ends (resolution) all contradictions.

1 | Promise	2 | Contradiction	3 | Resolution
*God's character preserves law and justice Exodus 34:6-7 *God is eternal 1:12 *God is in control by the power of His word. 3:1ff *God permeates creation 2:14	*To deal with Israel's violence, God sends more violence - His work is terrifying 1:5-11 *Habakkuk's situation changes for the worse *Will God remember to respond in mercy? 3:2 *Can Habakkuk respond with a heart of trust? 2:4	*God's knowledge and judgment will fall on Judah and people everywhere. 2:2-3 *Evildoers will be upended 2:6ff *God will deal with sin; people will see His holiness. 2:20 *Habakkuk survives and thrives firm in faith 3:16-19

Habakkuk's faith phases

Habakkuk's prophecy is delivered near the end of the southern kingdom of Judah when Nebuchadnezzar launches his first assault in 605 BC. Habakkuk's book is unique among the prophets. The other prophets present speeches for the general public. Habakkuk records his own wrestling in dialogue with the God of Israel.

Habakkuk knows God is a complicated mix of mercy and justice. The solution to the violence is voiced in the first few verses of chapter one. The people need to change their perverted behavior or God must change actions to prevent His people from continuing in sin. One contradiction rolls in when Habakkuk expects law and justice, but God announces more destruction and violence will be coming to deal with the evil. Expecting the people to change or God to change, Habakkuk learns it is he who must change and walk by faith.

Habakkuk appeals to God's eternity,, holiness,, and covenant promises. He trusts that God is in control by the word of his power. He appeals to God's righteous purity and jealousy to be worshipped. Habakkuk believes that God would not be true to his nature if he simply lets the Chaldeans have their way. Habakkuk waits confidently to see how God will receive his protest while hoping God does not forget to show mercy.

Yahweh assures Habakkuk that things will certainly change—but not until well into the future (Hab 2:2-3). He calls Habakkuk to trust his promise, even when everything looks and feels awful (Hab 2:4-5). Then he speaks of a time when all evildoers, everywhere, will be overturned. He does this by pronouncing five curses on the wicked (Hab 2:6-8, 9-11, 12-14, 15-17, 18-20).

Habakkuk's faith phases

Habakkuk arrives at two conclusions. 1. Habakkuk confesses it is terrifying to live between promise and reality, to live by faith (Hab 3:16). 2. He chooses to stand in faith, finding joy in God's salvation and strength no matter how much everything around him falls to pieces (Hab 3:17-19). This is a profound strategy while in phase 2 contractions: Manage faith, not the crisis.

There are two kinds of people living through tremulous times. One are the proud that trust in themselves and trust their material circumstances and the righteous who will live by their faithfulness to God. 2:4

We cannot change our circumstances. We cannot change the people around us. We cannot coerce change from God. But the one thing that must change in contradicting circumstance is us. We bank everything on God who is both willing and able to do all he has said he will do. This is what it means to live by faith.

Here is an example of how Jeannie Pace looked at the book of Habakkuk:

What's the Main Point or Generalization this Lesson makes About Reality in this Book of the Bible?

- Experiencing distress is the path to peaceful transformation.
- Distress proves faith.
- God's presence permeates creation

CHANGEPOINTS

I think I need to change my view of reality to match God's in the following areas:

- I need to wait on the wall 2:1 for correction. I need to be quiet so the Lord can say what is most important.
- I need to operate on a paradigm of generosity knowing God fills my needs and gaps.

Make a list here of other verses in the book that deal with God's view of reality

1 Habakkuk 2:4 We live by our faithfulness to God–not through our circumstances.

2 2:4 There are two kinds of people: Those that trust themselves and the righteous who live by faith.

3 3: 16-18 It is terrifying to live between a promise and the reality yet take joy.

4 2:14 The earth will be filled with an awareness of God's glory.

5 Mary, Martha and Lazarus experienced distress before peace.

6 The followers experience distress on the stormy seas before Jesus speaks peace into the storm.

7

8

For more information and generalizations from Dr. Strawn, see *RepresentationalResearch.com*.

His audio and video presentations appear on *Vimeo*.

CPSIA information can be obtained
at www.ICGtesting.com
Printed in the USA
LVHW040715221221
706908LV00008B/409

9 781088 011799